ANTI-ARRACK MOVEMENT OF WOMEN IN ANDHRA PRADESH AND PROHIBITION POLICY

ANTI-ARRACK MOVEMENT OF WOMEN IN ANDHRA PRADESH AND PROHIBITION POLICY

B. SARVESWARA RAO
G. PARTHASARATHY

HAR-ANAND
PUBLICATIONS PVT LTD

Har-Anand Publications Pvt Ltd
364-A, Chirag Delhi, New Delhi-110017

PRINTED IN INDIA

Published by Ashok Gosain & Ashish Gosain for Har-Anand Publications Pvt Ltd
Typeset at S.S. Computers and printed at Printline, New Delhi.

PREFACE

The anti-arrack movement of women in Andhra Pradesh was one of the most historic and significant movements of the decade of 1990s. It led to a commitment by the ruling party to adopt prohibition policy in the state.

The Institute of Development and Planning Studies (IDPS) thought it appropriate to bring together scholars from various disciplines to consider the implication of the movement and also to discuss the complex issues relating to prohibition. We bring together about dozen such important papers written by various scholars, in this volume.

Beginning in August 1992, in a remote village of Dubagunta of Nellore district in Andhra Pradesh, the agitation by women protesting against arrack auctions and demanding ban on the sale of arrack, spread like wildfire to almost all districts of the State. It is necessary to understand the problem in its proper historical and social context. It is equally necessary to recognise the implications of public policy on prohibition for State Revenue and also for employment. In view of the interdisciplinary nature of the problem encompassing historical, socio-economic, health, political, and financial aspects, there is a greater need for bringing people from various disciplines into a single forum for understanding the multi-dimensional nature of the problem. The IDPS has on its faculty academics drawn from several disciplines in an honorary capacity. It has also strong liaison with social workers and voluntary agencies.

The IDPS, therefore, felt it was appropriate to bring out a volume on the subject which could be useful in assisting public policy.

The following are the issues raised in this volume:

(a) Historical, Socio-Economic and Health aspects of alcoholism;

(b) Issues in public policy particularly regulation vs. prohibition and implementation; and

(c) Employment and revenue aspects of prohibition of alcohol.

The Institute of Development and Planning Studies expresses its grateful thanks to all the contributors for their great help in bringing out this volume. We hope this volume will be of considerable interest to all those who are interested in understanding the issues involved in the problem and effective implementation of prohibition in the State.

G. Parthasarathy

CONTRIBUTORS

1. Vavilala Gopalakrishnaiah
   Freedom Fighter, Veteran Gandhian,
   recipient of Padmabhooshan Award, and
   Hony. Advisor, Anti-Arrack Propaganda Committee,
   Govt. of A.P.

2. Prof. D. Narasimha Reddy
   Professor, Department of Economics,
   Central University, Hyderabad

3. Arun Patnaik,
   Centre for Economic and Social Studies,
   Hyderabad

4. S. Alwardas
   Ex-Minister, and President,
   Sri Srinivasa Vidya Parishad, Visakhapatnam

5. Dr. K.S. Krishna
   Hony. Fellow and Joint Director, IDPS

6. Kancha Ilaiah
   Reader in Political Science,
   University College for Women,
   Koti, Hyderabad

7. Prof. R. Venkata Rao
   College of Law, Andhra University, Visakhapatnam

8. Dr. Y. Satyanarayana
   Reader, College of Law, Andhra University,
   Visakhapatnam

9. Dr. P. Ramakrishna
Professor of Psychiatry,
Andhra Medical College,
Visakhapatnam

10. Dr. T.A.V. Narayana Raju
Professor and Head,
Department of Social and Preventive Medicine,
Andhra Medical College, Visakhapatnam

11. Dr. G. Ramachandrudu,
Professor of Economics, and Director,
Population Research Centre,
Andhra University,
Visakhapatnam.

12. Dr. B. Ratnakumari
Research Officer,
Centre for Women's Studies,
Andhra University, Visakhapatnam

13. Dr. B. Madhukar Patnaik
(Lecturer in Economics, IDPS),
Currently Lecturer in Economics,
G.V.P. Degree College, Visakhapatnam

14. Ch. Appa Rao
Research Asst., IDPS
Visakhapatnam

15. A.L.V. Kartikeye
Research Asst., IDPS
Visakhapatnam

CONTENTS

Section-I

ANTI-ARRACK MOVEMENT AND PROHIBITION POLICY IN AP

Section-II

ALCOHOLISM AND ETHICAL ISSUES

Section-III

HEALTH ASPECTS AND DE-ADDICTION OF ALCOHOLICS

Section-I

ANTI-ARRACK MOVEMENT AND PROHIBITION POLICY IN A.P.

1

ANTI-ARRACK MOVEMENT OF WOMEN IN ANDHRA PRADESH — AN OVERVIEW

B. Sarveswara Rao

Prof. G. Parthasarathy has clearly explained the issues raised in the Preface of this volume. The theme of this volume is basically concerned with issues relating to the ethics of development of Indian society within the framework of political democracy and the ideals of justice and equality, so clearly enunciated and embodied in our Constitution.

It would be most appropriate, if we could pay our tribute to the womenfolk of Andhra Pradesh, for launching the anti-arrack movement in the State. The movement brought to the surface, the agony and anguish of thousands of families who were being ruined every day by the evil of drink. The damage to the physical and mental health of the addicts as well as women and children of their families cannot be calculated in terms of money. I hope the great awakening of the women of Andhra, in respect of this social evil, would soon lead to an equally deep awareness regarding the disastrous results of other growing vices like cigarette smoking. The anti-arrack movement requires to be strengthened by all well-meaning people in the society. It needs to be institutionalised and converted into a powerful agency of voluntary action working at various local levels, for atleast a generation to come, so that the new ethos against drinking alcohol strikes firm roots. Even if the demands of the anti-arrack campaigners are agreed to by the State Government, there will always be the danger of the policy of prohibition being abandoned at a later date, unless there is continuing support for it from powerful voluntary action groups who have to act now with a sense of urgency. Whatever be the final outcome or impact of the anti-arrack movement on the State Government's policy, the movement has already done a great service to the society, reawakening it about the ethical and social values upheld by Mahatma Gandhi.

One might ask, if what is indicated by the trend of the anti-arrack movement is urgency of action in its support, why hold seminars of this kind? No doubt, there is some truth and validity in this kind of observation that we had enough of talking of philosophy and that it was time for action, as the issues concerned are alcoholism, promotion of human well-being and defence of human dignity. But talking philosophy is always a virtue. It helps to reaffirm faith in reason, to take cognisance of the full range of values involved—values relating to human freedom and dignity, equality and social justice and human development on the right lines. It helps to assess the consequences of action as well as organisational efficiency and the efficiency of means adopted for controlling the vice. In short, it helps to reaffirm our faith in reason, humanism and humanitarian principles.

I must confess, I am one of those who are extremely unhappy about the Excise Policy being followed by the Government of Andhra Pradesh during the last one decade. The Government's policy clearly reflected a deliberate and irresponsible disregard of the Constitutional provision relating to prohibition as made in the Directive Principles. The State went on actively boosting up production and sales of liquor, taking pride in the growing contribution of revenue by the Excise department to the State exchequer. The State Government made a mockery of the Directive Principles and the amendment of the Constitution 31C, intended to serve as an embargo on judicial interference in giving effect to the Directive Principles. Actually, it is the judiciary which seems to stand for the Directive Principles in a way interpreting the Fundamental Rights clauses while taking up some issues of public interest bearing on human rights, environmental protection, etc.

I believe that the implementation of prohibition policy by the State Government would firmly secure an important positive right or freedom for the people of Andhra Pradesh. I hope that the elevation of prohibition as a constituent of the Directive Principles and giving it the status of Fundamental Right would not face any fatal objections on grounds of economic capacity (calculated in terms of loss of Excise Revenue) or on grounds of administrative feasibility (difficulties in enforcing prohibition and controlling illicit trade in liquor). It is necessary to reaffirm that there is a strong case for prohibition in the context of the Indian situation particularly in Andhra Pradesh in the context of the situation prevailing now. The positive freedoms are now a days widely recognised as essential for enabling the citizens to exercise their basic political rights. True liberty or freedom implies a social order in which the claims of the citizens for equal opportunity especially the poor are satisfied, so that they can better exercise their political rights. The history of Liberalism in the western society, both as political philosophy and evolution of political process right from the beginning of the 19th century, clearly reveals a continuing and strong trend towards securing positive freedoms for the citizens. In our country too, there is a clear trend in this direction; and there are distinguished political thinkers, and members of the judiciary, like Justice Chinnappa Reddy, who are not happy that the Right to Work, Right to a Living Wage, Decent Conditions of Work, the Right to Education, continued to be merely Directive Principles and not Fundamental Rights. There is, therefore, no justification for the view that prohibition would involve abridgement of any fundamental right. The idea of a Welfare State implies that the State has the responsibility not only to take proper measures to mitigate poverty and destitution, unemployment, pollution of air, water and soils, etc. and to provide basic education and health care, but also to deny the citizens free access or free choice to consume goods injurious to personal and social health. The administrative and financial difficulties in implementing and enforcing prohibition could be easily overcome if there is a political will. It also appears to me that the social conditions are quite ripe in A.P. for prohibition now.

One question that is often raised in this connection is why not go for a policy of severe control and regulation of production, sale and consumption of alcoholic drinks instead of prohibition, with the clear objective of keeping down the levels of production and consumption of alcohol. My view in this matter is that effective control of the vice by way of drastic control and regulation would really involve virtual rationing of the quantities to individual consumers under licence, with additional regulation of the times and places where liquor would be available, measures for preventing resale of liquor by consumers, and presumably a reduction in the present prices of liquor to enable the poor consumer to minimise his expenditure on drink, which again means eradicating of excise revenues. I do not see any advantages in regulatory exercises of this kind in the case of alcohol industry and consumption. While the problems of controlling illicit manufacture and distribution of liquor would be serious in the case of prohibition, an effective combination of public management of prohibition, social control by strong voluntary action groups and health education would be a more successful strategy.

I do not suggest that the case for prohibition rested on moral grounds relating to purely personal conduct—on the ground that drinking is a sinful or immoral action or that it leads to neglect or indifference to certain accepted norms of moral conduct. The remedy in such case would really lie in promoting self-control through education and other means, though prohibition would help this process. It is, however, difficult to imagine "purely personal conduct" in the matter of alcohol consumption ignoring the consequences for the addict's family and the society. I am not also suggesting that the case for prohibition rested only or mainly on health grounds though in many cases the damage to health of the alcoholics is always substantial and significant, and warrants the drastic remedy of denying them totally opportunities for drinking. The damage to health in the case of smokers would be equally strong in many cases. I understand that in western societies many people die every year from diseases related to smoking tobacco and from diseases related to alcohol consumption. As a matter of general policy severe regulatory measures are needed to restrict consumption of both alcohol and tobacco. In the case of alcohol consumption in India, however, it is a far more serious social disease spreading fast to all sections of the society and undermining the Indian traditional feelings against habit of drink. The argument for prohibition, therefore, rested essentially on the enormous social cost of drinking and on the denial of opportunities it involves for millions of families for decent and healthy living. Prohibition would enable them, particularly the poor, to reallocate their limited resources for better living.

Prohibition policy will have to be treated as a basic component of need-based planning in the developing countries like India. It would be planning for the fulfilment of the basic needs with due recognition of the principles of humanistic psychology based on the theory of hierarchy of needs (Maslow's Theory) and the principles of humanistic economics which emphasise the developmental needs of the human being in directing the allocation of national resources to the various economic and social sectors and also the need for adequate control or regulation of the market forces. The State, while pursuing the policies of economic liberalisation with a view to encourage private enterprise, private initiative and other socially valid virtues, cannot and shall not give up its responsibilities to strive constantly for reallocation of resources both in the private and public sectors, in a manner consistent with the principles of humanistic psychology and economics.

The issue of prohibition can not be viewed in a narrow manner under any circumstances as a State fiscal problem. Even here there is no justification at all for the State to rely on the most regressive Excise levies and arrack auctions. There are more important economic, social and ethical aspects of alcohol production and consumption which need to be given adequate attention. The promotion of true human freedom and human dignity, welfare of the poor and the disadvantaged, and the overall development of the society on the right lines are the accepted national social goals, and the State policy relating to consumption of alcohol has to be consistent with these goals.

I am quite sure that this volume would be of great help in clarifying some of the issues I mentioned above and provide right guidance in the matter of implementing and enforcing prohibition.

2

REFLECTIONS ON ANTI-ARRACK MOVEMENT —PAST AND PRESENT—

Vavilala Gopalakrishnaiah

The women of Andhra Pradesh should be complimented for starting and sustaining the anti-arrack movement. The movement was started initially by the poor womenfolk of the Doobagunta village in Nellore District and very soon it spread to the whole of Andhra Pradesh and received wide support from the middle classes as well as intellectuals. The Press (especially the Eenadu Daily) played a notable role in educating its readers both about alcohol and the anti-arrack agitations. The political parties began showing interest as they could see some political gain in lending their support to the movement. The movement, no doubt, reflected the impact of the new mass literacy campaign particularly on the womenfolk. The social themes covered in the literacy primers used for instruction of the illiterates included the harmful effects of arrack drinking on health and well-being of the family. The sensitive *Story of Sita* in the literacy primers has been a powerful factor awakening the poor women of Andhra the victims of social diseases including alcohol drinking.

The demand for Prohibition in the earlier periods during the Gandhian era and later never became mass movement of the women victims as it is now. The cultural programmes carried out as a part of the mass literacy campaign organised by the Bharateeya Gnana Vignana Samithi, particularly the street plays, also contributed a great deal to the awakening of the womenfolk and led several of them to become activists determined to fight the social evil. Whatever be the final outcome of the mass literacy campaign regarding the levels of literacy and education, the impact of it on the social awareness of the people is bound to be durable and significant.

I recently visited the Harijan hamlets of the villages of Guntapadu and Vegurukhandu during my extensive tours in Andhra Pradesh. All the women of the hamlets said in one voice that as a result of their success in preventing their men from drinking they are now having sufficient food in the family whereas earlier the men used to come home every evening in a drunken state and often beat their wives and children.

The anti-arrack movement reflected also the struggle of the womenfolk for emancipation from the social forces of their degradation and for protecting their dignity. This is a movement of the poor and oppressed womenfolk unlike the earlier movements led by political leaders and elites. There was some risk of the movement dissipating into a sporadic and uncoordinated agitation and losing its momentum. The vested interests opposed to the movement, particularly the arrack contractors and dealers will attempt to weaken the movement by resorting to all methods. A new dynamic leadership would emerge as a result of this movement and would resist all such attempts with determination.

I recall an incident occurred in the Inamaduru village. The local arrack contractors offered to build a temple in the village at a cost of Rs. 20,000/- as an attempt to wean away the people from the anti-arrack movement. The villagers, however, realised that they are spending every year about Rs. 6.00 lakhs on arrack. If the villagers are keen to have a temple, a small one-time subscription from each family of the village would meet the cost of the temple.

Since the earlier State Government had realised that the movement was authentic and strong it introduced Prohibition without delay for the betterment of the society. The present State Government should also realise the need for complete Prohibition in the State. By adopting severe economy measures and by avoiding wasteful expenditure on entertainment, advertisement, populist cultural shows, unnecessary travels, etc. the Government departments could easily save substantial amounts to compensate for the loss of excise revenues. Apart from this, State trading in liquor is both unconstitutional and immoral.

The anti-arrack movement during 1920s was a part of the National Independence Struggle and demand for Prohibition. Picketing of toddy tapping and liquor shops and preventing liquor auctions were part of the non-violent and non-cooperation movements led by Mahatma Gandhi. However, these movements reflected more the urge for social and moral reforms by the leaders and did not become real people's movements. Also during the Gandhian era, the issue did not attract as much attention as some other issues of the Gandhian constructive programme such as abolition of untouchability and promotion of Khadi.

During the days of Salt Satyagraha Campaign in 1930s, cutting down of palm and date trees along with picketing of arrack shops were part of the Satyagraha movement. The Satyagrahi workers who used to cut down trees were subjected to considerable State violence and brute force of the contractors and were given more severe penalties and jail sentences by the Law Courts than other Salt Satyagrahi workers. As a result of the Gandhi-Irwin Agreement, however, the people's right to picket all liquor trade establishments was conceded.

In 1937 when the Congress Party formed the Ministry in the composite Madras Province, as per the 1935 Government of India Act, Prohibition was introduced in the State and in order to make good the loss of revenue resulting from prohibition, the Sales Tax was introduced. While it was widely recognised that due to Prohibition many families were benefitted unfortunately, there was no movement against the illicit manufacture of liquor which increased rapidly in 1941. During the Individual Satyagraha Movement, Gandhiji emphasised the 18-Point Constructive Programme which included demand for Prohibition; but again this did not attract as much attention as other issues such as communal harmony and national unity. In 1946 when Tangutoori Prakasam became the Chief Minister of Madras Province, Prohibition was introduced and when the separate Andhra State was formed in 1953, Prohibition continued to be in force in Andhra Districts and was not extended to Telangana. This made the implementation of Prohibition in Andhra area extremely difficult . The dual policy relating to alcohol consumption within the same State led to various anomalies and Prohibition was given up in 1960. During all these years, one could observe in retrospect, that no authentic grassroots movement' from the people, particularly the victims of the social evil, arose and there was no visible campaign against illicit manufacture of arrack which became widespread. Arrack money also became a big source of funds for corrupt politicians. The intellectuals hardly paid any attention to the issue of alcoholism and Prohibition. Several Expert Committees established for examining the issues recommended Prohibition to be introduced by stages; but the Governments thought only in terms of effective regulation of trade and consumption of alcohol.

A most astonishing and painful feature of State Policy in Andhra Pradesh has been the rapid growth of liquor trade and Excise revenues as well as revenues from Sales Tax which was imposed in 1937 with the main purpose of meeting the cost of Prohibition. The habit of drinking has been spreading rapidly to all sections of the society as there was no effective Government or social control, and arrack and liquor trade has also gathered more strength as a political force and started vitiating and corrupting the political processes. Fortunately, the present anti-arrack movement started by the poor rural folk and their demand for prohibition arose from the grass roots with tremendous awakening of the people, and perceived by the people themselves as social and political action required for protecting human dignity and securing social justice.

It is amply clear that the movement was not directed against the Government or any political party or the liquor contractors and dealers, and it was conceived in the true Gandhian spirit and philosophy of non-violence. As a women's movement, it has amply demonstrated that empowerment and legitimisation of women's struggles for equality and social reconstruction could be achieved in the Indian society by the women.

It is hoped that all the political parties, intellectuals and social activists would lend their full support to the movement.

3

ANTI-ARRACK AGITATION BY ANDHRA PRADESH WOMEN —A RETROSPECTIVE PERSPECTIVE—

D. Narasimha Reddy
Arun Patnaik

In the beginning of August, 1992, in a remote village of Dubagunta of Nellore district in Andhra Pradesh, the agitation by women protesting against arrack auctions and demanding ban on the sale of arrack, spread like wildfire to almost all districts of the State. The movement against the sale of arrack started in North Telangana districts like Warangal, Karimnagar and Adilabad at the behest of the CPI-ML (PWG in particular and other groups) but attempts were made to suppress it by the police intervention which went to the extent of selling arrack not only under police protection but even in the police stations. Notwithstanding the repression, there was a widespread people's ban on arrack sales in these districts and no auctions could be held for as many as 1739 arrack shops in 1990-91 in Warangal, Karimnagar and Mahaboobnagar districts. The CPI-ML sponsored ban on arrack sales was met by the State with brutal attacks on agitating women. The movement apparently started by the women, started spontaneously but in fact as a result of a combination of social, economic and political factors, was initially responded by the State with a kind of indifference under a cynical hope that it would fizzle out. This attitude of disdain bordering on scorn, could be seen from even the response of the English press. The movement was about two weeks old by the time newspapers like *The Hindu* and *Indian Express* started reporting. Starved of any important issue that would adequately capture the attention of the people a ride on the crest of which would be vote spinning, the anti-arrack agitation provided a ready bandwagon to political parties like TDP. The National Front leader NTR missed no time and converted the train journey to his film shooting located in Araku Valley near Visakhapatnam to address meetings by stopping the train even at unscheduled railway stations with scant respect to the inconvenience caused to other passengers. The CPI-M celebrated its involvement in the movement by conducting a National Seminar at Hyderabad through its front organisation Jana Vignana Vedika and provided a common platform, where almost all the parties including the Congress had exhorted the need for ban on arrack. The two-month old anti-arrack agitation in Andhra Pradesh was threatened with dissipation because of repression on the one hand by the State machinery and the hoodlums of arrack contractors, and on the other hand the gimmicks played by major opposition parties which were hardly involved with the movement at the grass-roots level.

To understand the movement with a view to strengthen it, one must place the problem in its proper historical and social context. The second part of this note tried to provide the recent historical background on the issue of prohibition and the third part draws attention to the mechanisms of penetration of the liquor largess into the political process denigrating the very democratic fabric of the Indian society. At the end an attempt is made to provide a policy outline as a response to the immediate context.

The Career of Prohibition as a State Policy

The early British policy relating to consumption of liquor, which was also interlined with excise revenue, was one of the temperance and of restricting the consumption of intoxicating drinks. One of the earliest policy pronouncements dates back to September 7, 1905, which stated that their 'settled' policy was "to minimize temptation to those who do not drink and to discourage excess among those who do, and to a furtherance of this policy, *all considerations of revenue must be absolutely subordinated.*" (Emphasis added). The policy of regulation and of discouraging the use of alcoholic drinks in excess continued till 1921, when with the introduction of the first Constitutional Reforms, the movement towards prohibition gained strength and resolutions declaring that prohibition was the ultimate goal of excise policy were passed by several State Legislatures.

Several State Governments apparently took measures to minimise the consumption of alcoholic drinks by the enforcement of controls on their manufacturing and distribution. But these measures do not appear to have had any salutary effect. In 1930-31 and 1932-34, as a part of the Civil Disobedience Movement there was picketing of liquor shops and toddy booths. The enforcement of complete prohibition, figured as the first item in the national demands submitted by Mahatma Gandhi to the British Government in 1931. He wrote in *Young India* in 1931, "...If I was appointed dictator for one hour for all India, the first thing I would do would be to close without compensation all liquor shops, destroy all toddy palms such as I know in Gujarat, compel factory owners to produce human conditions for their workmen and open refreshment and recreation rooms where these workmen could get innocent drinks and equally innocent amusements. For the loss of revenue from drinks, I would straight away cut down the military expenditure."

The Provincial Autonomy of 1937, which brought the Congress Party into power in several states, brought life to the programme of complete prohibition. Provinces like Bombay and Madras started implementing prohibition policy in stages. But the out-break of the World War II and the consequent resignation of Congress Governments in the states put a halt to the prohibition policy. Prohibition was lifted in all the states and revenues from excise soared high during the Second World War period partly because of the inflationary conditions. With the return of popular ministries in the States after the War, Prohibition was brought on to the agenda of action.

The World War II was an important turning point which brought the liquor revenue to the fore. It was during the Second World War period that revenue from excise, an indirect tax, became the single largest source, by passing the land revenue, a direct property based tax. In Bombay State, Excise receipts which amounted to Rs. 2.8 crores in 1938-39 increased by 1946-47 to Rs. 9.7 crores the single largest source of tax revenue yielding about 34 per cent of the total tax revenue. In Madras State, excise receipts increased from Rs. 3.8 Crores in 1938-39 to Rs. 16.8 crores in 1945-46, against Rs. 8 crores from land revenue.

Notwithstanding, the growing revenue presence of the excise duty, both the states introduced prohibition as soon as popular ministries assumed office in 1946. In Bombay a decision was taken to bring about complete prohibition in the State in gradual stages within three years time from April 1, 1947. Progressive reduction in consumption was ensured by the following:

(1) Closure of excise shops for 2 days in 1947-48, 3 days in 1948-49 and 5 days in 1949-50;

(2) Progressive reduction in the number of shops; and

(3) Reduction in the strength of liquor in the case of country liquor.

A separate law called the Bombay Prohibition Act 1949 was enacted and complete prohibition was brought about in the State with effect from April 6, 1950. Similarly, in Madras State soon after the resumption of power by the 'popular ministry,' the policy of prohibition was revised and by 1948-49, it was extended to all the districts.

Prohibition as an important state policy figures in the Directive Principles and Article 47 directs that the States "shall endeavor to bring about prohibition of consumption, except for medicinal purpose, of intoxicating drinks and of drugs which are injurious to health."

The task of extending prohibition as a national policy was considered as an important welfare measure and the responsibility for working out the modalities of the implementation of the policy was assigned to the Planning Commission. In 1954 the Planning Commission appointed a Prohibition Enquiry Committee (Shriman Narayan Committee) which submitted its Report in 1955. The Committee was very optimistic about the adoption of prohibition as a national policy and made a number of recommendations for a time-bound implementation. Some of the important recommendations of the Committee are;

i) that prohibition should be regarded as an integral part of the Second Five Year Plan;

ii) that the target date for completing Nation-wide Prohibition should be April 1, 1958;

iii) that in states which were yet to make a beginning and in the wet areas partial prohibition states, from April 1, 1956, there should be stoppage of drinking in hotels, bars, restaurants, messes, clubs, cinemas and in parties and functions;

iv) that there should be Prohibition Committee in each district and were upto the village and mohalla level;

v) that the Excise duties on narcotics and intoxicants

collected in the states are highly iniquitous, regressive and anti-social and this kind of levy has no justification to exist in a progressive tax system and should be wiped out at the earliest;

vi) that the Union Government would give adequate assistance to those states which depend on excise for a considerable part of their revenue to introduce prohibition in their areas; and,

vii) that a clear-cut statement may be issued by the Union Government to the effect that Prohibition has become a national policy.

As a sequel, the policy of Prohibition was discussed as a non-official resolution by the Lok Sabha which passed the following resolution March 31, 1956:

"This House is of the opinion that Prohibition should be regarded as an integral part of the Second Five Year Plan and recommends that the Planning Commission should formulate the necessary programme to bring about nation-wide Prohibition speedily and effectively."

The Second Five Year Plan included, as part of its 'social welfare services,' prohibition as an essential item of social policy. It emphasized that in the consideration of any basic social policy, financial considerations, although of great practical importance, are not to be treated as decisive in character. It suggested the following steps to be taken by the State Governments in wet or partially wet areas:

1. discontinuance of advertisements and public inducements relating to drink;
2. stoppage of drinking in public premises (hotels, hostels, restaurants, clubs) and at public receptions;
3. setting up of technical committees to draw up phased programmes with the object of:

(a) reducing progressively the number of liquor shops both in rural and urban areas;

(b) closing liquor shops for an increasing number of days during the week;

(c) reducing quantities supplied to liquor shops;

(d) progressively reducing the strength of distilled liquor produced by distilleries in India;

(e) closing of shops in and near specified industrial and other development project areas;

(f) removal of shops to places away from main streets and living quarters in towns and villages;

4. taking active steps to encourage and promote the production of cheap and healthy soft drinks;

5. assisting voluntary agencies in organizing recreation centres; and,

6. including prohibition as an item of constructive work in national extension and community project areas and social welfare extension projects.

One important step taken during the Second Five Year Plan was setting up of the Central Prohibition Committee by the Home Ministry and the Committee met towards the end of 1960 to review the implementation of Prohibition Policy. Otherwise, the action taken by the State Governments was not significant and the progress for the country as a whole was slow. One of the significant aspects of the Third Five Year Plan was to emphasise *prohibition essentially as a social welfare movement and recognition that if prohibition were to rest primarily on enforcement by the police and by excise staff not much progress would be made.*

"The main reliance has, therefore, to be on:

(a) the creation of a *growing public opinion* in favour of prohibition conceived as a social welfare measure in the interest of the general mass of the people;

(b) *voluntary organisations*, who should be given the necessary support and assistance by the Government in carrying out social and educational programmes;

(c) Implementation of various development programmes undertaken by government agencies in education, health, social welfare, etc. with due emphasis on the significance of prohibition; and,

(d) availability in canteens of cheap and nutritious food and non-alcoholic beverages and encouragement of sports, and recreational activities on a group and community basis.

"With a view to achieving greater progress in these directions, it would be useful to *provide financial assistance to voluntary organisations for educational and promotional work among the people* and also to give a measure of support to other activities which would assist the progress of prohibition." (Emphasis added).

Assigned with the task of devising the machinery and modalities for the introduction of prohibition as a national policy, the Planning Commission appointed in 1963 a Study Team on Prohibition under the Chairmanship of Justice Tek Chand. The Study Team submitted its Report in 1964.

For anyone dealing with liquor problem in India, Tek Chand Committee Report is a compulsory reading. Its informative and educative value is incomparable. The Comprehensive Report running into 1265 pages in two volumes covers almost every aspect of liquor manufacturing, trade, consumption, consequences, the history of the movements against liquor in India as well as abroad, the problems and failures of prohibition law. The only striking deficiency, a reader of 1990s would find is the absence of discussion, except in passing remarks on the situation in individual states of the corrupting influence of liquor trade on the political processes. One may explain it away either as a result of the terms of reference being different or because of the liquor-politics nexus by mid-60s not yet assuming such depths of degradation. Be that as it may, it need not detract one from the merits of the Report.

The most important recommendations of the Team include changes in the provisions of liquor laws, electoral disqualification of persons involved in liquor offences, mass education and publicity, active role for voluntary agencies and Nasha Bandi Lok Karya Kshetras throughout the country and a four-phased programme culminating into total prohibition preferably by January 30, 1970, the Birth Centenary of Mahatma Gandhi. But it was a cruel irony that during this period what really happened was quite the reverse—prohibition was lifted in almost all states, except Gujarat.

It is very perplexing as to how such a comprehensive report like the one by Justice Tek Chand met such a cruel fate. To unravel the mystery one should take into consideration the slow but sure changes in the nature of the emerging ruling classes, their social base and the compulsions of the coalition. Even as the Tek Chand study was being contemplated, the Uttar Pradesh Government abolished prohibition in eleven such districts where there was existing prohibition in 1964 but introduced certain dry days. Madhya Pradesh quickly followed suit. Mysore was the first State in the South to relax even its partial prohibition in 1964. Haryana scrapped prohibition in 1967 and Kerala did so in the same year. Orissa was the next to scrap prohibition in 1968. The Andhra area of A.P. followed suit in 1969. Assam liberalized prohibition in 1970. Maharashtra revised its policy towards a permit system. And with the abolition of prohibition in August 1971 in Tamil Nadu—hardly a year had passed since Gandhi Birth Centenary, there was no major State save Gujarat where prohibition was in force.

All observers of India notice that the mid-1960s marked a clear cut turning point for worse in the economy, polity and even in social policy as could be seen from the fate of prohibition policy. Not only were the otherwise much acclaimed recommendations of the Tek Chand Committee Report put to cold storage, even the Planning Commission which included prohibition as a part of the Welfare Programmes of the Second and the Third Plans, seems to have turned a cold eye. There is no mention of prohibition in the Fourth Five Year Plan document or the Annual Plans that preceded it!

The reasons for such a complete reversal to the 'prohibition policy' are not far to seek. These were closely linked not only to the economic and political changes but also with the subtle but perceptible changes in the very nature of the *ruling classes,* and their support base and means as well as sources of power. Of this the liquor excise revenue to the State and liquor contracts or illicit gratification to the *ruling classes,* make the reversal of prohibition policy a political necessity and of course a social scourge. Liquor emerges as a major source of revenue without displeasing the rich. What is more startling are the consequences. Let us first see how the turn around actually happened.

Ever since the formation of 'popular ministries' in the states in 1946, the pursuit of prohibition as a State policy was accepted but the action taken varied from that of complete prohibition in states like the then Madras and Bombay, partial prohibition in Uttar Pradesh and Madhya Pradesh, a policy of temperance in states like Bihar and West Bengal and no dry law in states like Rajasthan and erstwhile Hyderabad.

In most of the states which did not go in for prohibition, the policy of minimizing liquor consumption through maximum excise revenue ended up only in raising revenue instead of reducing liquor consumption. By late fifties, even in a State like Andhra Pradesh, which had parts without dry law, were moving towards revenue maximization, disregarding the very objective of curbing liquor consumption. The Andhra Pradesh Prohibition Enquiry Committee Report observed that "the objective of minimum consumption was not helped but vitiated by the objective of maximum revenue in which revenue was sought to be obtained from the poorest classes for being spent on society in general." The Report of the Taxation Enquiry Commission (1955-56) also observed: "...it is thus clear that the aim of reducing consumption has come to be ignored, and that though half a century has elapsed since the policy was first adumbrated, no tangible results in the direction of reducing consumption have flowed from the manner in which it has been in operation so far." But it was yet another irony that this Report of 1954 which produced recorded evidence on the failure of implementation of the dry law, instead of suggesting the ways and means of plugging the loopholes came out in favour of complete scrapping of the dry law! Needless to say that this committee had a mechanical administrative perspective devoid of either the history of such a measure in other parts of the world, or the historical context within India or the welfare implications involved in the issue. For such an effort, one had to wait for the Reports of Shriman Narayan and Tek Chand panels.

The strains of State's role, aided by certain natural calamities became quite apparent by the late 1960s. The State's role as a mobiliser of resources and as an investor faced severe constraints. The State investment registered deceleration. There was a threat to its role as an agency to legitimise the regime, the dominant coalition. Even the success of the Green Revolution in its early phase was throwing up its own contradictions as could be seen from mobilisation of farmers for higher prices and better terms of trade. The early avenues of public works contracts under the strain of resources were not proving adequate to harvest their riches. In fact, for the large majority of the land based politicians incomes are associated with harvesting notions and there is no other avenue that can harvest profits as quickly as contracts to the repertoire of which the liquor contract were added by the late 1960s.

Of the many factors, one that played a decisive role is the capacity of the liquor trade to quench the growing 'revenue' thirst of not only the states which were not willing to displease the affluent by taxing their growing wealth and incomes but also of the ruling elite who were looking for easy and quick sources to enrich themselves as well as to finance their election expenses which were reaching scandalous proportions incapable of being met by any hard earned incomes or party-funding, however, ingenious the mechanisms of mobilization might be. It is, therefore, interesting to note that the contribution made by any company to political parties was banned by legislation in 1970. State excise to the states and liquor contracts to the ruling elite or their henchmen, made politicians to look upon prohibition as utopian and far from being pragmatic. This stink of pragmatism in the polity was spreading all over, making a mockery of the democratic process. By late sixties and early seventies there was no shadow of doubt about the decadence and the entire political process was soaked completely in liquor largesse.

In 1973, the veteran Socialist leader Jayaprakash Narayan wrote: "money, falsehood, corruption and physical force have combined to erode steadily the very meaning and substance of elections. Election costs have been growing by leaps and bounds, and cases have been reported in which single state assembly candidate is said to have spent between Rs 30 and Rs. 40 lakhs and a Lok Sabha candidate spent between Rs. 60 and Rs. 90 lakhs. But even if the cost is one-tenth of these staggering amount, the poor man's party or candidate has no chance whatsoever.

"Nor can representatives capable of spending such large sums be ever expected to work for the poor. In the same way, the vice of impersonation, fed on secret funds, and the use of physical force, supported by powerful political and caste interests, have been growing at an alarming rate.

Corruption of the electoral machinery, commonly manifested in intimidation and buying up of presiding officers, has been growing apace alongside corruption in other fields."

The liquor trade which was considered as a social stigma up until late sixties and associated mostly with bootleggers, the criminals and anti-social elements, started acquiring political respectability with the growing dependence of the political elite on the money and muscle power of the liquor traders. The auction system in arrack and toddy, the rivalry in illicit distilling of arrack and smuggling of IML to avoid excise, gave rise to the maintenance of criminal gangs by the liquor contractors. The liquor contractors who were kept at an arm's length by the politicians earlier, started becoming their close allies to begin with, but soon the temptations and compulsions of the changing nature of the elections and the growing resource needs of electoral politics turned many politicians into liquor contractors as much as some of the liquor contractors graduating into politicians. Thus by the end of 1970's the criminalisation of political process gets rooted in the liquor and the very mention of regulation or control, leave alone prohibition, was met with ridicule and dispensed as non-pragmatic by all major political parties, in or out of power. The plight of the people who are the victims of the spreading tentacles of liquor and the liquor based politics hardly got any attention. It is in this context and anti-liquor movement of the women of Andhra Pradesh becomes all the more important. It is a major movement that can make the State to renege from the complete deviation from its own accepted policy.

The following section deals with three aspects of the women's movement against arrack in Andhra Pradesh. First, it examines the factors contributing to the deterioration of the very subsistence conditions and other facilitating factors that could be discerned as immediate circumstances causing the movement. Second, it provides a brief and sketchy description of the movement. And at the end cautions against the possible simplistic interpretation of the movement in terms of drunkenness as the cause and disciplining the male members of the household as the solution.

The Back-Ground of the Movement

By 1990-91, Andhra Pradesh occupied first rank in the country in arrack consumption. The other first rank occupied by A.P. is in terms of the total number of seats in cinema theaters. In recent years there has been a steep increase in the consumption of all kinds of liquor in the State. Table-1 shows that the arrack consumption in the State increased from about 54 million litres (300 U.P) in 1975-76 to 70 million litres in 1980-81 to 111 million litres in 1990-91. The consumption of IML increased almost five-fold in 1980s, from 4.4 million proof litres in 1980-81 to 219 million proof litres in 1989-90. Table 2 shows that though the share of sales tax in the total tax revenue increased from 44 per cent in 1980-81 to 52 per cent in 1989-90 and share of excise duty in the total State tax revenue remained around 28 per cent. The excise duty in absolute terms increased almost five times in 1970s from Rs. 35 crores in 1971-72 to Rs. 153 crores in 1980-81 and by almost six times in 1980s to reach Rs. 839 crores by 1991-92 (Budget Estimate). It is worthnoting from Table-3 that 70 to 80 per cent of the growing excise was accounted for by the revenue from arrack, the poor people's drink. Thus, the substantial burden of the regressive excise duty was borne by the poor. The number of arrack shops increased from 7,159 in 1969-70 to reach the peak of 22,803 shops in 1987-88 but declined to 16,436 in 1990-91. The decline in number of shops, in no way shows any decline in the arrack demand but reveals the ingenuous innovation in 1986 of arrack being packed in 90 ML and 45 ML polythene sachets. The introduction of sachets made mockery of the very concept of a 'shop' and the rental in relation to shops. Arrack in sachets started flowing to the doorstep by peddlers on foot and by bicycle. This innovation afforded the convenience of arrack being carried to any place and broke the association of arrack drinking with arrack shop. From the complaints of women of rural Andhra Pradesh, one could guess the damage it caused through increased drinking with little regard to place and the time of the day or night.

Liquor is one of those commodities that flouts all laws of economics, the increasing arrack consumption is accompanied by increasing price of arrack. The present price at which the State issued arrack to the contractor is Rs. 10.50 per litre 300 U.P. The "issue price" includes the cost, excise duty, transport charges, and bottling charges. The price at which the contractor sells to the `consumer in sachets of 90 and 45 ML or bottles of 180 ML presently works out to Rs. 50 to 60 per litre of 300 U.P., i.e., the difference between the sale price and the `issue price' works out to Rs. 40 to 50 per litre out of which the contractors have to meet the rentals which amount to about two-thirds of the total excise revenue. Of course, it one goes by the official data on arrack sales, the contractors don't seem to be big gainers!

For instance let us have a look at the A.P. official arrack consumption figures in 1990-91:

1. Total Arrack consumption	11.12 crore 30° U.P. litres
2. Sales Price at Rs. 55 per ltr.	Rs. 611.60 crores
3. "Issue Price" at Rs. 10.50 per ltr.	Rs. 116.76 crores
4. Gross Margin (2-3)	Rs. 494. 84 crores
5. Less Rentals for shops	Rs. 454. 00 crores
6. Gross Profits	Rs. 40.84 crores

These figures show a gross profit of Rs. 40.84 crores to arrack contractors in 1990-91. If one takes into consideration the maintenance expenses including the 'goonda gangs,' the bribes paid regularly to the excise department, the contributions to political parties and other miscellaneous contributions paid out of fear or favour, the contractors appear to be big losers! Everybody knows that the official statistics on arrack is a mockery of truth. Obviously, the consumption of arrack is much higher and this is accounted for by the extensive illicit distilling and packing parallel to the government arrack. And the resulting drain on poor people's income on arrack consumption in A.P. in 1990-91 could be at least double that of Rs. 611 crores of excise duty, i.e. Rs. 1200 crores. This one could believe is on the lower side.

Much of it is hard earned incomes of the entire households of the poor. Most of the drinking in rural areas is arrack and toddy. The proportion of arrack is much more. Most of the arrack drinking is done by the poor families most of whom are agricultural labourers. Though women do drink in Telangana region but they are largely confined to toddy. Caste-wise drinking is a social taboo among the upper castes and some groups of the backward classes. There is no social stigma attached to drinking of arrack or toddy by schedule castes.

In the 1980s the employment situation in A.P. has been worsening. There has been no substantial increase in wages. The prices of essential commodities like pulses, edible oil, tamarind and chillies have increased by 30 to 50 per cent during the last two years. The subsidised rice scheme though not properly targeted, did help the poor. One may criticise it as a 'left handed' charity because the State was taking away with other hand in the form of excise duty on arrack much more from the poor than what is given with the one hand by way of rice subsidy (Table-1). The Rs, 2 per kg. rice programme in A.P. was tampered by the Congress (I) government two years back and the price of rice for green card holders was increased from Rs. 2 to Rs. 3.50 per kg. and the quantity was reduced from 20 kgs to 16 kgs per family per month. These conditions are objective enough to make one perceive arrack as the major cause of ruin of the family life and living conditions of the poor and even the lower middle classes.

However, arrack trade and consumption have definite extra-economic dimensions out of which at least two are most important: one is social, i.e. the gender specificity of the suffering, and the other is political, i.e, criminal portends with its ramifications for the political and the civil life of the country. Invariably, it is the man who blows much of the household income on arrack and women of the household who has not only to struggle to provide for the subsistence of the children and the household and also end up at the receiving end of all the abuse and beating that often goes with the drunken male. The other part, i.e. the political part is the power wielded by the liquor contractors, their criminal activities and political nexus leading not only to loss the respect for political processes but also loss of hope of transformation for the better. It is in this context the demand for arrack ban by the CPI-ML groups during the last few years in North Telangana districts and the Women's movement starting-off in Nellore district acquired a spontaneity and spread all over the state.

The Events

While the post-literacy period in Tamil Nadu and Pondicherry seem to have ironically helped the BJP's newspaper to increase its circulation among the neo-literates, the Akshara Jyoti Programme assisted by the State and CPI(M), has a different historical trajectory in Andhra Pradesh, thanks to the radical politicisation of issues related to the women's struggles for survival. In Nellore, Chittoor and elsewhere, the neo-literate women in the villages pledged to fight against the "arrack demon" in the concluding sessions of the Akshara Jyoti programme. Since then a new momentum has been unleashed by the women over the last three months. To their credit it can be said that they have converted a women's movement to a people's movement which among other issues of class and state power is equally concerned with women's question.

There is echo of support for the CPI(ML) ban on liquor among the Nellore women who seem to have been inspired by it. Akshara Jyoti programme has also engendered an urge to survive with dignity—the dignity of labour—as also protect the household income against the 'arrack demon' so that their families can survive and they can educate their children. The neo-literate rural women's determination for survival for dignity of labour and for education of children has acquired new proportions. A Dalit Woman of Nellore said, "We will not allow arrack sales in our village even if they shoot all of us women. Better die once than die everyday."

The anti-liquor mass movement has not merely raised a woman question as being portrayed by the Press and a section of the intelligensia but also targeted its attack on the nexus between the so-called 'people's representatives', police and arrack contractors. When the women are demanding prohibition on arrack for a dignified survival, the people's representative in the State Government are busy in talking about the impending revenue loss in view of the prohibition. When the activists reply that the revenue problem is minimum because revenue can be generated through sales tax, commercial tax, etc. and that, in any case, during the post-prohibition period general consumption of commodities is likely to increase in urban and rural areas as well, the Congress Government retains its usual degree of quietism. In this sort of arguments, counter-arguments and more often the silence of the Congress Government on the on-going people's movement has unfolded its concerns to reform the family structures as well as exposed the class character of the excise policy of the ruling class parties, both the Congress Party and Telugu Desam Party.

The village committees formed in different villages are invariably led by the women belonging to the poorer Dalit households. These committees do not have any representations either from the Congress Party or Telugu Desam Party. This is true of most of the village committees, whether in the Coastal or Telangana Districts. In some villages as in Nellore, the upper caste women have only passive support for these committees. In other villages, like the ones in Ranga Reddy district, no upper caste women are even remotely concerned with the struggle against arrack contractors and police who are protected by the ruling Congress Party and the opposition Telugu Desam party. These committees, however, receive political aid and moral support from the State-level mass fronts, like Jana Vigyan Vedika (aided by the CPI (M)), the Progressive Organisation of Women (aided by a CPI(ML) group), and Andhra Pradesh Dalit Mahasabha. In Nellore district alone where the present mass movement has initially begun, the movement is organised by the Anti-Arrack Coordination Committee (AACC) comprising 36 voluntary organisations. In Chittoor district there are 250 voluntary organisations, active in the village committees comprising mostly women and youth spread over in more than 200 villages of the district.

Aided by these voluntary organisations, the village committees led by the women have pressurised their men to take oath in the village temples to stop drinking arrack. In case of violation of the pledge, the men would be forced to pay a heavy fine to the temple and the families would be banished from the villages. In some cases the wives have physically prevented their men from visiting arrack shops but are wondering how far could this tactic sustain when they (women) have to go for transplantation very soon.

In the villages, the women squads have discovered three instant instruments of struggle—broom, chilli powder and fire. They counter the threat from police and the drunken males with broomsticks and chilli powder. And they attack the contractors' dens and set fire to the barrels and sachets. These attempts symbolically aim at purification of their villages by burning the 'arrack demon.' The messages against the ill-effects of arrack on the household economy and against the nexus of police and arrack contractors are spread through graffitis street plays, rallies, door-to-door campaigns and public meetings in the villages. There is a beautiful graffiti which portrays how women are marching forward, breaking arrack bottles and how the contractors and police men are shell-shocked by this crusading spirit of the women. The women squads also prevent auction sales being organised by the Excise Department—a strategy initially adopted by the CPI(ML) Dalams. In Nellore alone, they have stalled auction sales thirty six times. This is true of almost all district auction counters. As a result, many women have been arrested and police have filed false cases against them. More and more such repressions are launched, the nexus between bureaucracy, police and arrack contractors are revealed before the agitating women. No wonder, the District Collectors engaged in such auction sales are sarcastically labelled as 'Indian Arrack Sellers' (IAS).

There are villages where women are guarding against sales of the arrack by squatting en masse in front of the liquor vendor's shops. They have been preventing peddling of sachets by bicycle or foot, often receiving not only rebuke but also beatings. Most of these women are agricultural labourers and many of them are from families where they are the main bread winners. Their work is seasonal and they are missing the season by keeping watch at the arrack shops. Their wages are too low to expect any possibility of falling back. Their menfolk have the habit of drinking with the wages earned by the women.

An Interpretation

As the movement against arrack unfolds itself, there are two important dimensions which became apparent. One is the determined bid by the state, particularly the police, the contractor's henchmen and the political parties, particularly the party in power, to dissipate the movement, and the other is the courage, valour and determination with which women are organising themselves against severe odds at the levels of villages. The police often resort to attack on the agitating women, prevent their meetings by denying permission wherever possible, and provide protection to sell arrack, sometimes resulting in selling of arrack within the police stations. The goondas, hired by the contractors are often found using abusive languages and attack on women in villages where they are vulnerable, and attempting to bribe certain sections to clandestinely or openly sell arrack in the vicinity of poorer households. The Government or the ruling party, Congress (I), has been trying to buy time in the name of gathering public opinion, hoping the delay would dissipate the movement. The only positive effect of the opposition party gimmicks appear to be putting fear of loss of votes and the consequent restraint on violent repression by the Government. But the skindeep commitment of the opposition parties is very well revealed by the total absence of any of their representatives at the village level committees formed by agitating women.

The women's struggle, on the other hand, took a number of forms by picketing in front of the arrack shops, in some cases confiscation and destruction of the arrack sachets, forming of 'battalions' of women who would keep watch in turns at the arrack shops, keep watch on the male members who are vulnerable to drink and on the arrack 'poachers' who would clandestinely enter the villages with sachets hidden in bags parading of male members who violate the ban imposed on arrack drinking. Closer at the household level there have been 'Broom Treatments' behind the closed doors and refusal to serve food for those coming home drunk.

These actions by the organised agitating women are very essential part of the movement and for rejoicing to mark happy events of their years of suffering and suppression. But any attempt to romanticise these actions may fall short of the objective of the educational process which it is supposed to serve. The suffering of the women, the very state of relationship between wife and husband, the absence of love and affection, within the household, the neglect of children and daily drunken brawls and the destruction of the very family life are adequate enough social indicators of the degenerating quality of life. It is the reflection of the shambles into which a nascent civil society is reduced and it is very much necessary to see its dialectical relations with the 'political society'. It is not enough if the women realize and agitate against the immediate cause—the arrack that is responsible for their miseries. It is much more important for them to see that their misery including arrack is perpetrated by the social system which needs to be transformed simultaneously but *without deviating from the immediate objective of ban on arrack.*

The Policy Perspective

The arena of policy relating to liquor is the most *treacherous* ground to *tread*. If the history of the anti liquor movements all over the world is any guide, it would offer one important lesson, i.e. *there is no one-time universal policy*. The policy if it were to be responsive to the interests of the people and safeguard people from any adverse manifestations, which there would be, should be based on certain specific duration or factor. One guiding principle is that it should be responsive to people's aspirations and needs. For instance, whether it was in the U.S.A. or Scandinavian countries or China, there has been prohibition or scrapping of prohibition and again reintroduction, but all the while with one objective of reducing, if not eliminating the evil of drinking and the institutions which go with it. Given the awareness of these aspects, what follows in this section should be seen as a response to the immediate context rather than a once for all prescription.

When it comes to outlining the course of action on the part of the State, with the hindsight of the ingenuousness with which even the constitutional directives have been flouted, there has been a lot of hesitation and even fear. The fear is that in the name of a policy of prohibition there could be unabated bootlegging under the aegis of the very agencies which are supposed to enforce it. These fears become all the more real given the present role played by the liquor and liquor money in the elections. But, with the people's movement and their proper involvement, one hopes for a better enforcement. Keeping this in view, the following suggestions are made:

Prohibition, if it should be successful:

i. should be introduced in phases;

ii. should be backed by public opinion and widespread education including the school, the public media and informal channels;

iii. should involve social workers, public minded persons, particularly women and voluntary organisations of proven record of good grass-roots educational activities; and,

iv. should have monitoring committees, particularly at the grass-roots level with the large women's presence to function as vigilantes or watchdog organisations with statutory power for enforcement.

The Tek Chand Study Team on Prohibition (1963) and the Third Five Year Plan make ample and detailed suggestions regarding introduction of prohibition in a phased manner. Prohibition may be introduced in two phases. In the first phase ban arrack, treat arrack in tribal areas differently, reduce the number of IML outlets to the minimum, let toddy be regulated and ban matka, single number and other forms of gambling simultaneously. Let us elaborate each of these measures:

(i) Arrack

(a) The sale of arrack should be banned throughout the State and involve large vigilance committees, at all levels, particularly at the village level with at least half the representatives from among women, in the enforcement of the ban. The enforcement should not be left to the police or excise department.

(b) Arrack and Adivasis or Tribals

As the Third Five Year Plan suggested in pursuing the programme for prohibition the customs and traditions of tribal people must be fully respected. The recommendation of the Tek Chand Committee needs to be given due consideration: "The adivasies or scheduled tribes with whom drinking is traditional may be allowed to brew such beverages to which they are accustomed for their consumption only ...a change has to be brought about in their mental approach and social outlook through more enlightened members of their community, than through persuasive law."

ii) Indian Made Foreign Liquor (IMFL)

(a) The number of IMFL shops/outlet should be restricted to atleast one-fifth of the present number. The shops should not be given to private trade but should be state owned outlets operating for limited number of days in a weak and limited number of hours in a day.

(b) In a State like Andhra Pradesh with an annual consumption of 111 million litres of arrack, one can not wish away that all arrack drinkers would stop suddenly in response to a ban. Introduce low duty cheaper IMFL which should be sold in limited quantity per person. This is based on Tamil Nadu experience, which may be improved by restricting the sale to only full bottles which would serve as a damper on poorer buyers. This is to wean gradually the hard addicts of arrack in the transition period and to check such persons taking to illicit arrack, which should be stamped out with peoples cooperation.

(c) The selling and serving of IMFL of more than 5 per cent alcohol content in all public places like hotels, restaurants, bars etc and public functions should be banned—a lesson from Tamil Nadu where prohibition is made a mockery by allowing large number of bars recently. There should be restrictions on location of IMFL shops in the vicinity of public institutions like educational institutions, religious places, State/National Highways etc.

iii) Toddy

Toddy need not be bracketed with arrack and IMFL. In view of the low alcoholic nature of the drink and its entraining the livelihood of millions of toddy tappers, toddy should be treated separately. It may be necessary to take a leaf from the Tek Chand Study Team's Report here:

"The toddy may be allowed to be served subject to the following safeguards:

i) A ceiling of 5 per cent alcohol in bulk should be fixed;

ii) The production and the sale of toddy should be under government control;

iii) Wherever possible, bottling to guarantee standard, and refrigeration to stabilize alcoholic strength should be provided;

iv) The drink may be consumed only at the place of sale and not be allowed to be taken home;

v) The quantity of toddy that can be served to an individual should be suitably limited and the vendor or barman should be under statutory obligation not to violate this condition;

vi) The price of toddy and the tax element, if unavoidable should be kept as low as possible with a view to dissuade people from drinking the hard product of illicit distillation;

vii) Drinking should be allowed only within regulated hours;

viii) Steps should be allowed only within regulated hours;

ix) The production and sale of toddy within a radius of five to ten miles of palm gur centres should be stopped; and

x) There should be an age limit of 21 years below which no consumer may be allowed or served the drink.

iv) Illicit Arrack, Drugs, Matka, 'Single Number' etc:

Banning of arrack doesn't automatically guarantee that poor people would switch their expenditure towards other domestic items like food, clothing, children's education, sanitation etc. that would improve the standard of living of the entire household. Several studies have revealed that a mere ban on arrack would not bring about the desired results if it is not accompanied by a similar ban and strict enforcement of laws relating to illicit liquor, matka, 'single number' game, drugs etc. towards which the poorer households are highly vulnerable.

Second Phase of Prohibition

The Second Phase of Prohibition should be one of continued campaign with all the sources of mass media against the adverse effects of not only alcohol but all kinds of drugs and narcotics. This phase should be based on the experience gained during the first phase, with adequate flexibility towards elimination of the possible distortions and deviations. Strengthening of education, public opinion and grass roots institutions against consumption of liquor should play a major role. It is essential to keep adequate room for debate, constant review for discussion, critical and continuous evaluation and modification. Only then the country can gear up to face greater problem that is looming large at the horizon, viz. the 'drugs'.

REFERENCES

Planning Commission, GOI, *Prohibition Enquiry Committee 1954 Report* (Shriman Narayan Committee) Delhi, Manager of Publication, 1955.

Planning Commission, GOI, *Report of the Study Team on Prohibition* Vol.I and Vol II, (Tek Chand) Delhi, 1964.

GOI, Report of the Taxation Enquiry Commission, 1955-56, Vol III, Delhi 1956.

Planning Commission, GOI, *Second Five Year Plan,* Delhi 1956.

Planning Commission, GOI, *Third Five Year Plan,* Delhi, 1961.

Table 1
Consumption of Different Liquors in Andhra Pradesh

Year	*Arrack*		*IML*		*Beer*
	No. of Shops	*Consumption (Million Litres) (300 U.P)*	*No. of Shops*	*Consumption (Million Proof Litres)*	*Consumption (Million Bulk Litres)*
(1)	(2)	(3)	(4)	(5)	(6)
1969-70	7159				
1970-71	8669				
1971-72	9294				
1972-73	9546				
1973-74	10745				
1974-75	12001				
1975-76	13847	54.4			
1976-77	13809	61.5			
1977-78	14154	63.4	1661	3.03	24.9
1978-79	14150	66.4	2998	4.4	74.2
1979-80	14135	67.1	4566	4.3	63.3
1980-81	13996	70.3	4321	4.4	44.0

Year	Arrack		IML		Beer
	No. of Shops	*Consumption (Million Litres) (300 U.P)*	*No. of Shops*	*Consumption (Million Proof Litres)*	*Consumption (Million Bulk Litres)*
(1)	(2)	(3)	(4)	(5)	(6)
1981-82	13847	69.7	3087	7.8	37.3
1982-83	16059	74.0	3698	8.9	38.4
1983-84	17643	83.3	4294	11.3	36.1
1984-85	18648	86.5	5941	10.5	37.9
1985-86	18949	88.7	5847	11.3	49.7
1986-87	22657	94.8	5381	14.2	45.8
1987-88	22803	103.7	5344	18.6	37.0
1988-89	16772	117.2	6072	15.5	46.2
1989-90	16426	116.1	6503	21.9	46.9
1990-91	16436	111.2	6744	18.1	49.9
1991-92	16507				

Notes: Rounded off to nearest crore.
Source: Reports of the Comptroller and Auditor General of India (compiled by Dr. V.J. Naidu, S.V. University).

Table 2

Excise and Other than Tax Revenues of A.P. (Rs. Crores)

Year	State Excise	*Land Revenue*	*Stamp duty & Regstrn.*	*Sales Tax*	*Taxes on Vehicles*	*Others*	*Total*
1979-80	141 (28.6)	32 (6.48)	28 (5.68)	217 (44.00)	49 (9.94)	26 (5.27)	493 (100.00)
1980-81	153 (26.29)	33 (5.67)	35 (6.01)	279 (47.94)	53 (9.11)	29 (4.88)	582 (100.00)
1981-82	194 (27.60)	34 (4.88)	41 (5.83)	342 (48.65)	58 (8.25)	34 (4.84)	703 (100.00)
1982-83	235 (29.08)	26 (3.22)	44 (5.45)	402 (49.75)	64 (7.92)	37 (4.58)	808 (100.00)
1983-84	282 (29.22)	14 (1.45)	45 (4.66)	497 (51.50)	80 (8.29)	47 (4.87)	965 (100.00)
1984-85	351 (29.82)	18 (1.53)	53 (4.52)	607 (51.75)	93 (7.93)	51 (4.36)	1173 (100.00)
1985-86	417 (29.98)	21 (1.46)	69 (4.79)	761 (52.88)	113 (2.85)	58 (4.07)	1439 (100.00)
1986-87	448 (29.74)	13 (0.88)	74 (4.75)	803 (51.51)	128 (8.21)	93 (5.97)	1559 (100.00)

Year	*State Excise*	*Land Revenue*	*Stamp duty & Regstrn.*	*Sales Tax*	*Taxes on Vehicles*	*Others*	*Total*
1987-88	499	16	92	971	143	98	1819
	(27.63)	(0.88)	(5.06)	(53.38)	(7.86)	(5.38)	(100.00)
1988-89	565	42	107	1107	167	134	2122
	(26.63)	(1.48)	(5.04)	(52.17)	(7.87)	(6.31)	(100.00)
1989-90	660	33	124	1237	193	137	2384
	(27.65)	(1.38)	(5.20)	(51.89)	(8.08)	(5.75)	(100.00)

Notes: (i) Rounded off to nearest crore
(ii) Figures in parantheses are percentages

Source: Reports of the comptroller and Auditor General of India (compiled by Dr. V.J. Naidu, S.V. University).

Table 3
Excise Revenue from different Liquors and Rice Subsidy Andhra Pradesh

(Rs. in Crores)

Year	*Country Spirit (Arrack)*	*Country Fermented Liquor (Toddy)*	*Malt Liquor (Beer)*	*Foreign Liquor (IMFL)*	*Others*	*Total Excise Revenue*	*Rice Subsidly*
1971-92	5 (16.24)	17 (48.57)	0.4 (1.14)	2 (5.71)	10.06 (28.74)	35 (100.00)	—
1972-73	6 (17.68)	18 (52.94)	1 (2.94)	2 (5.88)	7 (20.59)	34 (100.00)	—
1973-74	7 (15.90)	19 (43.18)	1 (2.27)	4 (9.09)	13 (29.55)	44 (100.00)	—
1974-75	36 (62.07)	17 (29.31)	1 (1.72)	3 (5.17)	4 (1.72)	58 (100.00)	—
1975-76	53 (69.74)	16 (21.08)	1 (1.32)	4 (5.26)	2 (2.63)	76 (100.00)	—
1976-77	70 (72.16)	16 (16.48)	2 (2.06)	6 (6.19)	3 (3.09)	97 (100.00)	—
1977-78	76 (73.79)	16 (15.53)	2 (1.94)	7 (6.80)	2 (1.94)	103 (100.00)	—
1978-79	91 (75.83)	15 (12.50)	3 (2.50)	9 (7.50)	2 (1.67)	120 (100.00)	—

Year	*Country Spirit (Arrack)*	*Country Fermented Liquor (Toddy)*	*Malt Liquor (Beer)*	*Foreign Liquor (IMFL)*	*Others*	*Total Excise Revenue*	*Rice Subsidly*
1979-80	109 (77.30)	15 (10.64)	5 (3.55)	9 (6.38)	3 (2.13)	141 (100.00)	—
1980-81	118 (77.12)	19 (12.42)	5 (3.27)	8 (5.23)	3 (1.96)	153 (100.00)	—
1981-82	151 (77.84)	27 (13.92)	4 (2.06)	10 (5.15)	2 (1.03)	194 (100.00)	—
1982-83	179 (76.17)	17 (7.23)	21 (8.94)	16 (6.81)	2 (0.43)	235 (100.00)	—
1983-84	220 (78.01)	19 (6.74)	10 (3.55)	25 (8.87)	8 (2.86)	282 (100.00)	110
1984-85	265 (75.50)	37 (10.54)	8 (2.28)	25 (7.12)	16 (4.56)	351 (100.00)	160
1985-86	322 (77.23)	30 (7.19)	10 (2.40)	33 (7.90)	22 (5.28)	417 (100.00)	135
1986-87	348 (77.68)	27 (6.03)	30 (6.70)	30 (6.70)	14 (3.13)	448 (100.00)	189
1987-88	410 (82.16)	38 (7.62)	8 (1.60)	28 (5.61)	15 (3.00)	499 (100.00)	191
1988-89	475 (84.07)	36 (6.37)	8 (1.41)	39 (6.90)	7 (1.07)	565 (100.00)	169

Year	Country Spirit (Arrack)	Country Fermented Liquor (Toddy)	Malt Liquor (Beer)	Foreign Liquor (IMFL)	Others	Total Excise Revenue	Rice Subsidly
1989-90	526 (79.69)	48 (7.27)	8 (1.21)	75 (11.36)	3 (0.45)	660 (100.00)	302
1990-91	556 (76.37)	53 (7.28)	13 (1.79)	102 (14.01)	4 (0.55)	728 (100.00)	366
1991-92 (B.E.)	608 (72.47)	48 (5.72)	18 (2.15)	160 (14.07)	8 (0.60)	839 (100.00)	406
1992-93							256

Notes: (i) Rounded off to nearest crore.
(ii) Figures in Parentheses are percentages.
(iii) 'Others' include commercial and denatured spirits and wines, and toilet preparations containing alcohol, opi.

Source: Reports of the Comprtoller and Auditor General of India (compiled by Dr. V.J. Naidu, S.V. University) Col. 8 A.P. Budget Documents for relevant years.

4

NATIONALIST MOVEMENT AND GANDHIAN MOVEMENT AGAINST ALCOHOL

S. Alwar Das,
K.S. Krishna

The problem of alcoholism is not a new problem. Drink was considered as "vice" and "immorality" during the course of history. Some writers considered the habit of drink as the undesirable legacy of the savage life and the remnant of slavery. Physicians associated the problem with the medical aspects of human living and the morbid conditions that result from alcoholism. The harmful effects of drink on domestic budgets was a problem for investigation by researchers during the last century. The pioneering studies of household budgets in England, undertaken by Seebohm Rowntree, had revealed that the real sources of "Secondary Poverty" were "drinking, betting and smoking."

In the Indian society consumption of alcoholic drinks is an age old habit. According to researchers, 48 varieties of intoxicating drinks were in vague in ancient India. However, it cannot be deemed that alcoholism was approved by society. Kautilya dealt with the problem of intoxicating drinks in his Arthashastra and recommended prohibition of drinking in army camps. Even in ancient times writers and administrators suggested that liquor shops should not be located in crowded localities and necessary steps should be taken to avoid temptation to drink. During the course of history, number of attempts were made to implement prohibition programmes by the rulers in our country. Although drinking alcohol was not a taboo except in the case of certain religions like Buddhism, several Hindu and Muslim rulers before the advent of British rule abstained from drinking alcohol. Fa-Husien, who visited India during Gupta period reported that the people did not drink intoxicating liquor. Allauddin Khilji had introduced prohibition in the city of Delhi. Spirituous liquor was forbidden. Tippu Sultan introduced prohibition of some kind in Salem district and other parts of the then Mysore State in 1780. Drinking alcohol was an exception with the majority of the masses; it was despised.

The problem of alcohol seems to be an intractable problem today as it was so during the course of history. Attempts to control drink habit through prohibition programmes could not be implemented for long periods. No doubt, the problem has become more complicated because of change in the outlook from traditional to modern, erosion of moral values, increasing activities of the State, and the political overtones the problem has acquired. In a developing and democratic society, the problem has been transformed into a problem of national economy, government policy and social reform. Nevertheless, the socio-economic upliftment of the masses is still the primary objective of the State policy. It is in this context knowledge of the prohibition programmes adopted during the Nationalist and Gandhian Movement will be useful. The Nationalist leaders accepted prohibition as the integral part of action programme for the achievement of freedom because of their concern for moral values, Indian sentiment and economic upliftment of the masses. An in-depth study of the anti-alcohol movement and the programmes of prohibition adopted by the Nationalist and Gandhian Movement would shed light on the intricacies of the problem. We believe such a study would provide better insights and help to draw meaningful conclusions which may serve as lessons at the present juncture.

Excise—The British Policy of Non-Interference and Its Impact

The advent of British rule in India was marked by a systematic attempt to introduce some of the measures that were in vogue in the United Kingdom mainly for getting revenue. Excise duties on alcoholic liquor which gave substantial revenue prompted the East India Company and its successor British Government to introduce excise laws in India. These laws were enacted in 1790 as policy measures to obtain "maximum revenue with minimum consumption."

At the beginning of the 20th century, the manufacture of country spirits developed into a major industry and excise on the country spirits constituted half of the total excise revenue. The Government formulated its guidelines of excise policy for the guidance of provincial governments in September 1905 and these guidelines categorically stated that it had no intention to interfere with the habits of the persons who used alcohol in moderation, and it was its duty to make provision for the needs of such people. It was interested in getting maximum revenue without "stimulating illicit consumption to a degree" which would drive people to consume harmful form of liquor.

One of the terms of reference assigned by the Government to the Indian Excise Committee of 1905-06 was to find out an efficient distillery system. The British Government was interested in changing the then existing "out still" system because under this method taxation of manufacture of liquor was not quite feasible and it could not give more revenue.

The policy of maximum revenue with non-interference in the alcohol habits of the people aimed at promoting moderation. The Government had no intention to interfere in the liquor habits of the people because it considered such interferences as outside the duty of the Government.

The introduction of the new system led to the establishment of large number of private distilleries and as a result the production of country spirits and beers developed into a roaring industry. There was increase in the consumption of both locally manufactured and imported spirits. Indubitably, the British people influenced the consumption habits of the locals in respect of alcoholic drinks. The impact of the new system was disastrous on tradition, moral values and social customs because the restraint exercised by these forces slowly but surely gave place to new forces. The trade interest of the alien Government strengthened these forces. The anti-social nature implied in the consumption of arracks was forgotten and drink acquired social acceptance. The situation was further aggravated by increasing urbanisation and other allied factors. That increased taxation would reduce the consumption of alcohol was proved wrong. At this jucture Gandhiji entered into the National Movement.

The Gandhian Movement Against Alcohol

The Nationalist Movement in India was an outcome of large number of factors, and the most important was the British imperialism. The formation of Indian National Congress in 1885 marked the beginning of an organized effort by the people of India against this imperialism. The new organisation asserted itself as a Nationalist Movement by organising agitation against the partition of Bengal, under the banner of Swadeshi Movement, which forced the British Government to revoke the decision in 1911. The Nationalist Movement could not maintain unity among the various classes who demanded different approaches for the Freedom Movement. There was uncertainty with conflicting groups holding different opinions regarding the tactics to be adopted which led to the Surat Split in the Congress organization in 1907. The British Government offered the Minto-Morlay reform package in 1909 to secure the co-operation of Nationalist Congress leaders, moderates and extremists. The out-break of the First World War in 1914 proved to be a set-back for the fight against imperialism because it helped to rally the opinions of the Nationalist Movement in India "around the defence of British Empire." The leaders of the Nationalist Movement believed that their demand for political autonomy would be considered by the British Government after the war.

Gandhiji, a leader of "epic stature" returned to India in 1915 and acquainted himself with the Nationalist Movement by undertaking an extensive tour of the country and getting advice from Gopal Krishna Gokhale. He was convinced that the Excise Policy served as an instrument not only to fill the coffers of the British Government but to undermine the moral values, tradition and social customs; it acted as an obstacle to social and economic upliftment of the masses. Immediately he took steps to launch a campaign with the twin principles of Satya and Ahimsa. Even during the war Gandhiji began experimenting with his Satyagraha Movement which was a landmark in the history of freedom struggle.

Demand for Total Prohibition

The end of the First World War marked the beginning of a new era; the Nationalist Movement under the leadership of Gandhiji was given a new direction with the preparation of an action programme. In 1920 the Indian National Congress demanded the abolition of liquor and drug shops under the guidance of Mahatma Gandhi and pledged itself to total prohibition. Thereafter, total prohibition became one of the chief planks of Nationalist and Gandhian Movement along with eradication of untouchability and other projects. "Prohibition was not a reform in isolation, but one of the most important items" of action programme.

The Montford reforms of 1921 enabled several Provincial Governments to enact local optional laws, which was a recognition of "the principle of self-determination on the part of local bodies in the matter of restricting the sale of intoxicating liquor within their respective jurisdiction;" but the policy failed to reduce the consumption of liquor. Measures to reduce drinking in a particular area resulted in a rise in consumption in the neighbouring areas. Illicit distillation and smuggling increased. The demand for total prohibition gained momentum. In several provinces resolutions were passed by Legislative Councils that prohibition should be declared as the ultimate goal of excise policy. In 1925, in the Central Legislative Assembly, a similar resolution, moved by a non-official member, was passed. Thus considerable pressure was brought on the British Government for accepting prohibition.

The year 1929 marked the beginning of a renewed struggle for freedom under the leadership of Mahatma Gandhi. The historic resolution for Purna Swaraj was passed at the 44th Session of the Indian National Congress, held under the presidentship of Jawaharlal Nehru at Lahore (December, 1929). It was in this session the Congress resolved to approve a scheme prepared by C. Rajagoplachari for the prohibition campaign. The prohibition scheme*[1] consisting of 15 specific items underscored the role of Congress Party for the implementation of the programme at the District and Taluk levels. A notable feature of the scheme was organization of anti-drink processions and sabhas, and pledges to be taken in writing from voters and citizens supporting total prohibition.

Civil Disobedience Movement and Prohibition

In the year 1930 freedom struggle entered into a new phase with the launching of Civil Disobedience Movement for Purna Swaraj. Gandhiji had enlisted eleven items and requested the Viceroy of India (IRWIN) to satisfy the vital needs of India as a condition not to proceed with the Civil Disobedience Movement. The very first point was total

1. See Appendix for the Scheme.

prohibition. At the time of breaking the Salt law, which began on March 12, 1930, Gandhiji gave a clarion call from Dandi to fetch ornaments and contraband salt, to picket liquor shops, foreign cloth shops and opium dumps, and to launch a movement against untouchability.

The 45th Session of the Indian National Congress held at Karachi in March, 1931 noted with satisfaction the "progress of the Nation towards total prohibition" during the previous 12 months and called upon the organization "to continue the anti-drink and drugs campaign with renovated vigour" and hoped that the women of the country would redouble their efforts "in weaning the drunkard and drug addict from a habit that ruins both body and soul and desolates happy homes." The Karachi Session also passed a resolution on fundamental rights and it was in this resolution prohibition was referred as one of the items, emphasising that intoxicating liquor and drugs be used only for medical purpose. The call given by Gandhiji had a tremendous influence on both men and women throughout the country and they continued to picket liquor shops with great zeal and fervour, and went to the extent of cutting the toddy and palm trees. This movement against alcohol continued for a considerable time.

The Civil Disobedience Movement was resumed in January, 1932 after the return of Gandhiji, "empty-handed" from the Round Table Conference held in London in 1931. As a result of prolonged Disobedience Movement and arrest of thousands of satyagrahis and leaders, the Foreign Government came out with a new constitution which was adopted in 1935. This Act envisaged a new phase in the growth of National Movement, bringing together, according to historians, "the three discordant forces," the Congress organization representing the majority opinion, the minorities and the princely states. The Constitution provided for a federal polity. This gave an opportunity for the nationalist forces to form provincial Governments and take necessary steps for the implementation of a programme of reconstruction and social reform for the upliftment of the masses.

Prohibition Programme by the Nationalist Congress Governments

At the beginning of 1937 the Congress fought provincial elections and got majority in seven provinces and formed Ministries. Subsequently, it formed coalition Government in Assam. Non-Congress Governments came to power in three other provinces[1]. The Congress Working Committee meeting held in Wardha in 1937 appealed to the Ministries in the Provinces and also to the Indian states to adopt the programme of prohibition for the moral and social upliftment of the masses. For the first time in British India total prohibition was experimented. In the words of Coupland, British Scholar, prohibition was the "most striking social reform which only Congress Ministries attempted with genuine ardour and on a substantial scale" which was one of the most cherished projects of Gandhiji.

In this context it must be mentioned that there was some opposition to prohibition mainly on financial reasons. Gandhiji observed with a deep moral conviction that drink and drugs revenue was a form of degrading taxation. "All taxation to be healthy must return ten-fold to the tax-payers in the form of necessary services. Excise makes people pay for their own corruption, moral, mental and physical." "The removal of such degrading tax would enable the drinker to earn and spend better so that it would be ultimately a substantial economic gain to the nation."

Implementation of the Programme

Total prohibition was first introduced in the whole of Salem district in September, 1937. In Madras the ardent advocate of prohibition, C. Rajagopalachari wanted speedy

1. * See Table 1.

implementation, but financial considerations came in the way. Similar to what we find today, excise duties had been one of the main sources of provincial revenues and they constituted 17 per cent of the total. In the case of Madras the proportion was higher at 25 per cent. Despite the financial considerations prohibition was extended to Chittor and Cuddapah districts on October 1, 1938. It was felt by the people that prohibition would bring about improvement in the material and moral condition of living in the area.

Initially, the Bombay Government introduced prohibition in three rural areas. An ambitious scheme was drafted to cover the whole province in three years. The programme was launched in Bombay city with great enthusiasm and demonstration. The most important feature of the prohibition policy implemented by the Bombay Government was the levy of a tax to compensate partially for the loss of excise revenue; it levied a tax of 10 per cent on the "letting value of houses and lands in urban areas." This perhaps may be emulated by the present day Governments.

In the case of United Province (U.P.) series of steps were taken to implement the policy. Total prohibition was introduced in two districts. Etah and Manipuri, the number of excise shops in the remainder of the province were reduced by 25 per cent, substantially higher retail prices were fixed, some liquor shops were managed directly by the excise department, hours of consumption were fixed and rationing was imposed.

In the case of Central Provinces (C.P.) prohibition was first introduced in some selected districts and towns. The sale and import of some of the intoxicants were totally prohibited.

In the Bihar Province prohibition was introduced in 1938 in selected areas initially in respect of one or more excisable articles. A vigorous propaganda on the need for temperance was carried on.

In Orissa where addiction was common among Harijans and labour as "an escape from abject poverty and sickness," and the Government decided to tackle the problem of opium addiction which was wide-spread in the Balasore district. Number of other measures such as closing excise shops located in prominent places, ban on the sale of intoxicants after sunset, abolition of the practice of carrying liquor home and discouraging the sale of toddy were introduced.

In the North West Frontier Province (N.W.F.P.) an Ordinance was issued in November, 1938 prohibiting the manufacture, sale and consumption of intoxicating liquors and drugs, and it was implemented only partially in a single district.

In Assam the Congress-led Coalition Government introduced total prohibition of opium in the sub-divisions of Dibrugarh and Sibsagar in 1938.

Impact on Excise Revenue

Comparison of provincial excise revenues of 1939-40 with those of 1936-37 which was attempted by Coupland (See Table-1) had shown a decline in all the provinces with Congress Ministries where the prohibition programme was implemented. In the case of Bengal and Punjab Governments where the programme was not implemented by the non-Congress Governments excise revenues actually increased.

It comes out of Table-1 that the decrease in excise revenue was the highest, that is, about 33 per cent in the case of Orissa province, and lowest, that is, about 9 per cent in the case of Central Province. The excise revenue of United Province also recorded a striking decline of more than 23 per cent after the introduction of prohibition programme. The two provinces where the decline in excise revenue was substantial (U.P. and Orissa) were also the provinces where the programme had greater coverage, with a variety of measures and rehabilitation programmes undertaken for the success of the policy. The consumption of excise intoxicants in U.P. declined in some places by 40-50 per cent

Table 1
Provincial Excise Revenue 1936-37 and 1939-40

(Rs. in lakhs)

	1936-37	*1939-40 B.E.*	*+ or - over 1936-37*
Congress			
1. Bombay	325	287	- 38
2. Madras	396	355	- 41
3. United Province (U.P.)	153	116	- 37
4. Bihar	116	103	- 13
5. Central Province (C.P.)	64	58	- 6
6. Orissa	33	23	- 10
7. N.W.F.P.	9	9	0
Congress-led Coalition			
8. Assam	36	31	- 5
Non-Congress			
9. Bengal	136	157	+ 21
10. Punjab	104	111	+ 7
11. Sind	35	35	0

Source: Kishori Mohan Patra: The First Congress Ministries: *Problems and Prospects (1937-39), in, A Centenary History of the Indian National Congress (1885-1985), Vol. III*, All India Congress Committee and Vikas Publishing House Pvt. Ltd., P. 188 quoted from R. Coupland, *Indian Politics*, P. 142.

The Congress Ministries which implemented the programme faithfully could not find alternative source of revenue to balance their budgets. Some of the Provincial Governments especially the Bombay Government had an intention to appeal to the Centre to save them from "bankruptcy." Gandhiji who was also concerned with the problem came out with some "radical" ideas without any hesitation; he suggested reduction of educational budget for which the excise revenue was the main source until then. Measures such as short-term loans to tide over the situation were also suggested. Gandhiji wanted to approach the Central Government with a plea to curtail the military budget so that the amount may be utilised for giving proportional grants to Provinces.

Benefits from the Programme

The Congress Governments made experiments in the implementation of several other projects during their short period in power. Number of laws were enacted for the benefit of the common people. Upliftment of Harijans, educational programmes (adult education), land revenue remission to agriculturists, etc., were some of the projects undertaken. Statistical information on the benefits resulting from the projects, in terms of cash value to the people, was provided in the annual report of General Secretary of the Congress Party for the year 1939-40. Particulars relating to prohibition programme are given in Table-2.

It is evident from the figures that the net annual benefit was the highest in the case of Bombay and the lowest for the Central Province. The differences in the net benefits may be due to difference in coverage of area under the prohibition programme, different types of measures taken to reduce the consumption of liquor, and also due to the steps taken for rehabilitation. Although the figures in the table substantiate the argument that the programme resulted in net cash benefits, unfortunately figures are not available for the loss incurred in the case of U.P., and for both loss and benefits in the case of Orissa, the two provinces where the programme was implemented with a variety of measures. Further, information is not available on the procedure adopted in arriving at these estimates.

Table 2
Benefits from Prohibition

	Loss to Govt.	*Benefit (cash value per annum)*	*Net *Benefit*
1. Bombay	180	500	320
2. Madras	65	260	195
3. United Province (U.P.)	—	100	—
4. Bihar	20	60	40
5. Central Province (C.P.)	9	27	18
6. Orissa	—	—	
7. N.W.F.P.	—	—	
8. Assam*	4.5 *	—	

* Calculated

Source: A.M. Said and Dr. S.G. Zaidi (eds), *The Encyclopedia of India National Congress, Vol. XII: 1939-46*, S.Chand Company Ltd., New Delhi, p. 281 to 284, also see *Centenary History*, op. cit., PP. 214 and 215.

Additional information is available on the economic results of prohibition in the Madras State from a study undertaken by Thomas in 1939, the then Prof. of Economics, Madras University. In fact, the study was undertaken on the suggestion of the Government for examining the economic effects of prohibition in the Salem District. The results of the survey, based on study of family budgets in the Salem town and four villages had shown that the drink was not the principal cause of poverty but an aggravating factor atleast among working classes. The meagre incomes of the people were further attenuated by drink, leading to debt, disease, litigation and family disorders. The study also concluded that there were many exceptions to the enforcement of prohibition. Several people were given permission for the use of liquor, people usually crossed border areas to places where there was no prohibition, illicit distillation and use of unhealthy spirits were not uncommon etc. But prohibition committees which were appointed for the purpose of implementation did good work and the Police Authorities discharged their duties with vigilance. The study observed that although it was difficult to assess the effects of prohibition within a short period of one or two years, the programmes implemented in the district improved efficiency in production but increased the earnings of factory workers only to some extent. It is significant that the study had brought out the psychological reactions of the addicts to prohibition. It also observed that the results depend upon the general economic conditions prevailing in the State.

The experiments in prohibition and other social reforms produced good results during a short period. The report on the 52nd Session of the Indian National Congress observed that in the case of Bombay Province "the public, especially the poor, gained about Rs. 7 crores annually for only three items, namely, prohibition, labour and land legislation."

The Congress Working Committee meeting reiterated its stand to resolve the implementation of social reforms at its Wardha Session held in October 1939. But within a month, i.e., in November, 1939, the Ministries had to resign at the out-break of the Second World War. The Congress Working Committee at its Wardha meeting strongly protested against the Viceroy's (Lord Linlithgow) declaration that dominion status "was the ultimate objective of the British Policy in India" but the future set up was to be decided at the end of the war. The Congress Ministries in the provinces had resigned "in protest against the declaration of the war by the Viceroy without consulting provincial governments and the reluctance of British Government to give India Independence." The social reform movement was revived only in 1946.

Conclusions

An attempt has been made in this section to arrive at some conclusions on the experiences of prohibition during the Nationalist Movement. It is hoped that these conclusions would help us to draw lessons for the existing situation.

The excise system introduced by the British Government was based on the principle of maximum revenue with least interference in the consumption of intoxicants by the people. Manufacture of alcohol increased, the industry gained prosperity and drink acquired social acceptance.

Gandhiji and other National Leaders considered the excise policy as anti-social and against the Indian sentiment. During the Gandhian Movement drink was considered as a vice and immorality. Prohibition was not a reform in isolation but an important item of Constructive Action Programme during the Freedom Movement.

The policy of enacting "local optional laws" for controlling the habit of drink did not fructify. Therefore, the demand for total prohibition gained momentum in twenties. It may be drawn from this that the introduction of prohibition in some specified pockets may lead to bad practices.

Prohibition was given highest priority at every phase of Nationalist Movement. The appointment of separate committees to look after projects under social reform and the preparation of a detailed scheme for prohibition by C.Rajagopalachari brought out the sincerity of purpose and strength of conviction. These approaches underline the need for a detailed preparatory work for the introduction of the programme.

That prohibition became one of the moral planks of the Civil Disobedience Movement for Purna Swaraj in thirties, and the sustained struggle for total prohibition until its achievement in 1937 justify the conclusion that the cause of prohibition was something like a crusade during the Gandhian Movement.

The Congress Governments accepted the implementation of prohibition as a challenge. The main difficulty in implementing the programme was financial. But the measures taken by the Bombay Government, especially the imposition of a tax on the "letting value of houses and lands in urban areas" may be emulated.

Gandhiji's observation that a healthy taxation system should return ten-fold the necessary services contains some element of a good tax system. Measures undertaken for compensating the loss in revenue may be based on this principle.

The experiences gained during the Nationalist Movement with regard to the implementation of prohibition programme justify the conclusion that the problem requires the introduction of a variety of measures simultaneously for its success. Rehabilitation measures have to be taken to tackle physiological and psychological problems resulting from prohibition.

The effects of a policy like prohibition of intoxicants cannot be assessed in a short period. As observed by Thomas in his study of Salem district, the immediate impact may be unfavourable especially on habitual drunkards and the results may not be pronounced.

It comes out of the experience during Nationalist Movement that the poor and very poor households resort to greater consumption of intoxicants because of higher incidence of poverty. The effects are closely related to the prevailing conditions of employment especially in agriculture and other programmes of social reform.

The contents of this paper are also a source of two basic issues. Do we consider drink as immoral and a blot on our civilisation? Is prohibition demanded because drink is against Indian sentiment or because prohibition brings about economic upliftment of the masses? The answers to these questions will help us to understand the differences in approaches between the Nationalist Movement and present movement. Yet, the experiences gained during the Nationalist Movement are useful today.

REFERENCES AND NOTES

Samuel Smiles considered the habit of drink as the remnant of the Savage and Survival of Slavery. See, Herman Levy: *Drink, An Economic and Social Study*, Chapter-III, London, 1951.

Seebohm Rowntree: *The Human Needs of Labour, London* 1937. Rowntree defined Secondary Poverty as a standard of life of families living in poverty even though their earnings would be sufficient for the maintenance of physical efficiency.

O.M. Prakash: *Food and Drinks in Ancient India*, Oriental Booksellers and Publishers, Delhi, 1961, pp. 298-301. The author described the preparation of 48 varieties of intoxicants.

R.Shamma Sastry: *Kautilya's Arthasastra*, Book-II and Book-X Mysore, 1923.

Sacchindra Kumar Maity: *Economic Life of Northern India In the Gupta Period*, pp. 68 and 117, quoted from, *The Report of the Study Team on Prohibition*, Vol. II (Tek Chand) Planning Commission, Government of India, 1964.

Ishwari Prasad: *History of Medieval India*, Foreword by L.F. Rushbrook William, Delhi.

For historical background of prohibition in Salem District, see P.J. Thomas: *Economic Results of Prohibition in the Salem District*, Madras, 1939, p. 5. After Tippu Sultan's attempt to introduce some kind of prohibition in 1780 in the Salem District, the Board of Revenue selected Salem District in 1875 for the introduction of improved excise system. In 1929, the experiment of prohibition was tried in 3 taluks of Salem District.

Report of the Prohibition Enquiry Committee, 1954-55 (Chairman, Shriman Narayana), Planning Commission, Government of India, Delhi, 1955, pp. 4 and 5.

Ibid., pp. 6 and 7.

In the levy of excise, the "outstill" system was prevalent over greater part of the country during the early years of British rule. This system included "all systems prior in order of development to the levy of a still-head duty. The states of development were farming of large areas to individual bidders for excise purposes, farming the small areas, sale of the right to distill and sell at a particular place and lastly, sale of a similar right subject to control of means the time for distilling." The articles chosen for levy or regulation were distilled country spirits or arrack. Thus excise revenue was derived mainly by means of specific duties on excisable articles. eg. "still-head duty in the case of country liquor and Indian made foreign spirits. See *Ibid*, pp. 5 and 9.

The right to manufacture, distill and sale was given to highest bidders "without placing any restriction on the number of shops or quality of the spirit manufactured." See, *Report of the Study Team on Prohibition*, (Tek Chand) op., cit., p. 392.

The Bengal Excise Commission appointed in 1884, "noticed an increase in the consumption of intoxicating liquor" and felt that the main reason was the effect of social, moral and religious changes as well as relaxation of restrictions." See, Report of the Study Team on Prohibition (Tek Chand), *Vol. II*, Ibid, p. 394; and also see, *The Prohibition, Enquiry Committee* (Sriman Narayan), Ibid, pp. 9 to 13 for a discussion on the increase in consumption and the fallacious statements of Blackett, Finance Member in 1925.

D.C. Gupta: *Indian National Movement*, Vikas Publications, 1970; and V.D. Mahajan: Fifty Years of Modern India (1919-1974) Chapter-II, pp 113-251.

A Centenary History of the Indian National Congress (1885-1985) Vol. III, All India Congress Committee & Vikas Publishing House, (Pvt.) Ltd., Preface, Delhi, 1985.

Ibid.

Report of the Prohibition Enquiry Committee, op, cit., p. 14; and, *A Centenary History of the Indian National Congress, Op. cit.*, vol. II.

Ibid, pp 15 and 16 (Report).

The Encyclopedia of the Indian National Congress, Vol. IX, (ed). A.M. Zaidi and S.G. Zaidi, p. 649-651, and also see, *Centenary History, Vol. III, op. cit.*,

Ibid, Vol. III and also Vol. II (Centenary History).

The Encyclopedia of Indian National Congress, op-cit., Vol-X p. 146. For Gandhiji's ideas on Women, see, S.R. Bakshi: *Gandhi and Status of Women*, Criterian Publications, 1987.

V.A. Narain, in *Centenary History, op. cit., Vol. III*, The Act of 1935: Impact on National Politics (Chapter-I)

Coupland: *Indian Politics, London*, 1943, quoted from, Kishori Mohan Patra: The First Congress Ministries: Problems and Prospects (1937-39) in, *A Centenary History, op. cit.*, (Vol. III), p. 183.

Ibid, p. 184

The Government of India Act of 1935 empowered the provincial Governments to legislate with respect to intoxicating liquors and narcotic drugs.

Particulars of prohibition programme implemented in provinces by the Congress Governments are drawn from, *A Centenary History, Vol. III, Op. Cit.*, pp 184 to 187.

For Information on other programmes, See, *The Encyclopedia of Indian National Congress, Vol. XII*, op. cit., and also *A Centenary History*, Vol. III op. cit. P.J. Thomas, op. cit.

See, *The Encyclopedia of the Indian National Congress, Vol. XII*, op. cit.

A Centenary History, Op. cit. Vol. III, 212 and 213.

APPENDIX: PROHIBITION SCHEME

The following scheme for the prohibition campaign prepared by C. Rajagoplachari was approved:

1. Each provincial Congress Committee shall appoint a Prohibition Sub-Committee or put a single person in charge in order to prosecute the anti-drink-and-drug campaign in the province, and set aside sufficient funds for the purpose.
2. The Sub-Committee or member in charge in each province shall call for honorary workers who are willing to organise the campaign for prohibition in the taluqa. The Provincial Sub-Committee shall thereupon select from these one worker for each Taluq, provided that the Sub-committee shall have power to change the secretary if it deems necessary.
3. The organising secretary of each Taluq shall proceed to form anti-drink sabhas in as many towns and villages of the Taluq as possible, enrolling as members all persons sympathising with the object viz., the eradication of the drink and drug evil and the enactment of laws for total prohibition. Members of these sabhas need not be members of any Congress Committees or habitual weavers of khadi.
4. Attached to every such Anti-Drink Sabha and subject to its control shall be organised a volunteer corps into which shall be enrolled men and women ready to render honorary active service strictly adhering to the principle of non-violence and carrying out the instructions issued from time to time by the provincial sub-committee and the taluq secretary.

5. On the second Sunday of every month meetings and processions shall be organised against the use of intoxicating drugs and drinks demanding total prohibition.
6. Besides the holding of the above monthly meetings it will be the duty of primary organisations and the taluq secretary to hold as many gatherings as possible in their respective areas and organise village to village and house to house visits for combating the evil within their jurisdiction.
7. Anti-Drink Sabhas and Congress Committees shall organise wherever possible healthy counter attractions at such places and hours as may be suitable in order to divert people from the drinking habit.
8. At each anti-Drink meeting, pledges shall be taken in solemn form from all persons promising to abstain from alcholic drinks and drugs.
9. Sabhas may, after obtaining the sanction of the provincial sub-committee, organise peaceful picketting of liquor and drug shops wherever the same may be usefully done by their volunteers.
10. Sabhas shall exercise their influence to prevent landholders and lessees from letting out their trees for tapping for manufacture of intoxicating drinks.
11. Sabhas shall dissuade people from bidding at auction sales for the right to vend drinks and drugs.
12. On or before the third Sunday of every month each taluq secretary shall gather information and send a brief report to the provincial sub-committee of the meetings held on the preceding Sunday and other work done during the previous month in his taluq. The provincial sub-committee shall

consolidate these reports and send them to the Working Committee and to the Press for publication.

13. Written pledges shall be taken from voters and citizens supporting total prohibition in the following form with name and full address legibly written:

"I hereby pledge myself to support the enactment of laws for the total prohibition of intoxicating drinks and drugs as indispensable for the moral, economic and social welfare and progress of our country. I further declare that in any election to local bodies and provincial and All-India Legislative bodies I shall not vote for or support any candidate who has not signed the pledge in support of total prohibition."

Suitable books for taking these pledges shall be distributed by provincial committees.

14. The Provincial sub-committee may appoint a district prohibition secretary when the amount of work within the district calls for such appointment.

15. If and when elections to the Legislative Councils and Assemblies are held and Congressmen participate in them the introduction and active promotion of total prohibition shall be made a part of the election pledge of Congress candidates.

It was resolved that a Central Committee consisting of C. Rajagoplachari, Convener, Dr. Ansari, Dr. Rajendra Prasad and Vallabhabhai Patel be formed to give effect to this scheme. Resolved further that a sum of Rs. 500 per mensum for the next nine months be sanctioned for prohibition work and Rajagoplachari be requested to send a monthly progress report.

(Source: A.M. Zaidi and Dr. S.G. Zaidi (eds): *The Encyclopedia of Indian National Congress, Vol. 9,* S. Chand and Company Ltd., New Delhi, pp. 649 to 651).

5

ANDHRA PRADESH'S ANTI-LIQUOR MOVEMENT

Kancha Ilaiah

Rural women in Andhra Pradesh are making history. Illiterate women—whose minds and bodies appeared to have been crippled under the heavy weight of hard labour, landlord and market exploitation, social and domestic oppression, and who have been 'public goddesses' and 'private sex objects'—have now suddenly revolted against their husbands, the mandal officer, the police sub-inspector, the Collector, Superintendent, Home Minister and Chief Minister. Their demands are simple—'no drinking or selling liquor'. Drunkards are being dragged into the street, their heads clean-shaved; the liquor dealers are being brought into the 'chowrasta' garlanded with chappals and onions and made to over ride a donkey and taken round through the village. In hundreds the women go to the nearby police station to tell the sub-inspector the bitter truth, "You are only licking the boots of 'sara' contractors." They go to the local landlord, whose very presence spelt terror to them not so long ago and say "stop trading with our men's blood and our honour." They go to the collector, who, of course, will be in the company of the SP to warn him "either stop auctioning 'sara' or dare to drive your car over our bodies." They go to the Chief Minister carrying a letter written in blood of a young woman to demand "ban liquor or bury us all." The methods that they use are neither Gandhian nor Marxian but uniquely their own. In some villages when the landlord—contractor goondas came to attack women campaigners they retaliated with 'lathis.' The landlords, their drunken goondas and even the police have now realised that these women have turned into 'Kalikadevis' (Kalis).

Listening to these stories and watching the men with shaven heads paraded before us, we (a four-member team which visited the areas in Kurnool district) thought that we had reached a 'pramadavanam' (the women's world) where the unbelievable is happening. I have never been a witness to such a convulsion in village society before.

Kurnool is the home district of the then Chief Minister Vijaya Bhaskar Reddy. From Kurnool, Srishailam is 175 km. cutting deep into Nallamala hill forest range. The road takes us through two wild animal sanctuaries. One, a human 'animal' sanctuary, the second, a lion's sanctuary. The human sanctuary consists of different landlord-liquor contractors who rule the roost. There are three ferocious landlord-contractors in the area. The area between Kurnool and Srishailam is 'their sanctuary'. Unlike the lions which live in the sanctuary that extends from Atmakuru to Srishailam, these human 'animals' use guns, goondas without any fear from the State or any other agency. In these sara arrack baron kingdoms any ordinary mortal who speaks a word against them will be killed and fed to the fish in the tank and the fattened fish is eaten. One of them is known for using the expression 'champi chapalakesta' (I will kill you and feed the fish) and few escape him. But the anti-liquor women's movement has shaken the foundations of this World.

How it Began

The movement started as a result of spillover of the Nellore liquor movement and proceeded to stop the auctioning of liquor shops at Kurnool through protests, 'dharnas,' human road blocks to stop the Collector and the

SP from reaching the place where the liquor auction was supposed to take place, etc. These illiterate women were led by an educated women called Sandhya (Vice President of a progressive organisation for women, Stree Vimukti), who is called 'akka' (sister) by all. For the landlords Sandhya is like Draupathi, couragious and confident, and wants nothing but a war with them till the liquor business and landlordism is put to an end. It is for this reason that one of the landlords sent his drunken 'Dussasanas' to disrobe her and the rest of the women campaigning against liquor at Bangla near his native village. But the women fought back. The women who never figured in the political discourse of the State suddenly found a definite place. Not only do women call the women-activists as Akkalu, so do the men, both the politically conscious and not so conscious.

The Kurnool movement has a rhythm of its own. Having realised the potential of the women in Nellore district who stopped the auction, and subsequently too, the Kurnool women activists decided to stop the auction that was supposed to start. They succeeded in their first attempt and it was postponed further. The women again gathered in front of the Collector's office to stop the auction and it was again postponed, but this time with the decision to start the auction early morning. Friends of the women's movement within the administration, leaked out this information and women reached the collector's office at 3 am. The shocked officials and contractors then decided to take up more deceptive mechanisms. In the face of the threat to cancel the auction, the officials and contractors arrived at a compromise and the cut-throat (earlier the Kurnool's landlords and contractors killed each other) competition was turned into a friendly distribution of 'addas' (liquor markets) among themselves and instead of auctioning the shops, the concerned contractors were asked to sign the contract agreements secretly at their houses or in the hotels. The State machinery at the district level was reduced to such a face that in the presence of the landlords the officials could do nothing but shiver.

The women decided to fight the conspiracy in their own way. Since they were deceived (but not defeated) at the district headquarters they chose their villages as battle grounds.

Take for example the fisherwomen of Sundipenta and Lingala Gattu, two villages on the right bank of river Krishna adjacent to Srishailam barrage. Their men catch fish from morning to evening and drink liquor in the evening. The 200 odd fishermen of Lingala Gattu were estimated to consume liquor worth Rs. five lakh every year.

For these drunken men cheating and beating women was a daily routine. Education was something unknown. In the rainy season they drink only the muddy water that flows in the Krishna and while there has never been clean water, they have always been supplied with 'clean liquor.'

These women, after participating in the dharna at the collectorate, decided to stop the sale of liquor in the village. The contractor of the mandal, who is known to be a friend of the C.M. and an arch rival of another contractor decided to sell liquor in the village at any cost. After secretly signing the contract he promptly brought two truckloads of liquor to the Sundepenta-Lingala Gattu adda, in the early hours of October 2, Gandhi Jayanthi day. By then the women had developed their own intelligence network and as they got information about the trucks, ran to the outskirts of the village and stopped them. The police too had rushed there promptly but with instructions not to let loose terror but wait and watch the women. The contractor refused to take the trucks back and the women refused to leave the spot. For two days and two nights are women kept the trucks there. They mobilised stocks of rice, vegetables and cooked there. Their children were put to sleep in 'jholas' hung from trees. On the third day the SI of Srishailam again deceived the women by telling them that the liquor would be dumped at godowns but would not be sold. But after three days the liquor packets reached the sales counters of the villages. The women promptly rushed there and destroyed the packets. The police then arrested them and filed cases against 26 women. The women were let off on bail by the Atmakur Magistrate but Section 144 was also imposed from then on in Sundipenta.

Meanwhile, the Chief Minister visited Srishailam Mallikarjun temple and the Sundipenta women decided to seek from him a promise to ban the liquor. In hundreds they reached the guest house with a memorandum written by their leader and a poem written in blood to say "we do not need liquor that drains our blood." Despite the police, they reached the CM and asked him to read the memo and 'give his word' to ban liquor. However, the CM told them that the could not do so. The women simply decided to sleep across the door and not let the CM go. The panic-stricken police had to mobilise large numbers of women police to remove them and make way for the CM. Having fought public officials at all levels the women realised that everyone was deceiving them and the better course of action would be to focus on reforming their men and the local shops.

On Home Front

The struggles of the women on the home front are more significant than their fight against the State. As usual they requested their men not to drink. Since most of these habitual drinkers have already become psychological wrecks they did not care. The women decided to meet out symbolic punishment. Even this collective decision could have been resisted by the men but for the fact that they saw how each wife had turned into a Kalika—the wife who was eating his beatings every day was now facing the SI, CI, SP, Collector and even the CM. The local landlord-contractor, who was a terror to them became 'adanavadu' ("its only him") both at the Collectorate and in their village. All this has shaken the confidence of 'drinking husbands' who used to beat their wives.

At Kistaraopet the women's collective declared that those who drink would have their heads shaved and those who sold liquor would be taken round on a donkey. No man dared to say 'no' to the declaration. First, because it would amount to supporting drinking which has suddenly become a 'shameful' act. And each wife saw this as an opportunity to set her husband right.

At Kistaraopet a liquor shop-owner, in spite of threats sold the liquor and some 'dare devils' bought and drank it. Hundreds of women went to the seller's home, dragged him out, garlanded him with chappals and onions and took him round the village in a procession. It is mandatory for every working class woman to participate in the procession. They caught hold of the drunken men and they themselves shaved their heads in the presence of hundres of villagers. The moment a stranger visits the village, all the women surround him/her, and tell them all they have achieved.

Earlier, in one of the contractor's 'kingdom' women could not dare to criticise him but now they publicly talk of how he has been terrorising men and women of that area. The 'speak bitterness' campaign of the women leaves none untouched—the husband, the landlord and the police. It appears as though the village women's gatherings have started a 'small cultural revolution.' This is what shocked the village men. It is, however, wrong to think that there are no men to support the anti-liquor struggle. Conscentious and educated youth lent support. Interestingly enough the village women did not allow the enthusiastic men to out-shadow them while dealing with officials or while narrating the events. In our presence, Mallika, the local activist of Sundipenta, asked a youth leader to shut-up while he attempted to intervene. They are very conscious about their leadership, their strength and weakness. When an MP, a faction leader, asked them while they were talking to the CM to "set their husbands right so that the problem gets solved" they replied "when your wife could not set you right how can we set our husbands right."

For the women, liquor represents economic and health problems. One after the other the women talk of how the families' economy was being ruined due to liquor—they point to a man sitting around them and say "this man was drinking Rs. 40 worth liquor a day. He sold an acre of land, all his wife's ornaments and all the grain procured for food." Another woman said that she became a widow at the age of 30 because of liquor. Another woman pointed to a boy of 12 years and said his father taught him drinking. "Now I cannot think that the liquor devil dies even with his father's death", says she. Not that the diehard drunkards do not come to public gatherings with their pet theory that 'with drinking I could forget the day's labour and the body aches.' They do. But the women retort, "They drink by propping up this bodyaches theory and beat us so that our bodies keep on aching day in and day out." They say 'a drunken man does not eat ordinary food but wants 'neesu' (mutton or fish, etc.) which we can never buy because of his drinking.

The social complications that emerge from drinking are no less. Women cited example after example of how some one misbehaved with his mother or sister. The women in these areas sit at the liquor shop to keep a watch on selling and drinking because the police have said "we do not bother if you control drinking but we will intervene if you destroy liquor packets." So they simply sit and keep a watch. But this is a 'speak bitterness' gathering. Every woman criticises her drinking husband and exposes the economic problems due to liquor consumption.

State Response

The State and the ruling parties do not seem to be interested in what is happening at the family and the village level. Of course, many 'big' leaders stand disturbed by the fact that the women were prepared to face the goondas sent by liquor campaigning. To attack the campaigners they were ready with chilli powder and lathis to retaliate. The 'problem', according to them, is going far beyond liquor—the women are becoming powerful. The very atmosphere in the State—that there is a strong class movement, anti-caste dalit movement emerging—is enough reason for the landlord forces to be afraid of and the women's movement as an added dimension.

The State is attempting to divert the discourse to budget statistics—how to mobilise Rs. 860 crore revenue loss from banning liquor. Their real worry is about the unstated income which works out to Rs. 2,500 crore per year. For every 25 paise that the State gets, the contractors get 75 paise. Part of this huge amount gets back to political parties in the form of party funds. With the anti-liquor movement the present form of election system would be in a crisis because 'liquor-packet-distribution and vote-mobilisation' is an integral part of the electoral game. Of course, the situation in the State was such that, every party, except the Congress, was promising prohibition to capture rural women's vote. The Governor, Krishnakanth and his wife, Suman Krishnakanth, were busy preaching morals to anti-liquor agitators—no violence, no politics, etc.—while they themselves live amidst the politics of Raj Bhavan and were heading the violent State machinery which were organising attacks on agitating women day in and day out. The areas under the grip of Naxalite groups—Nizamabad, Adilabad, Karimnagar, Warangal and Khammam where actually anti-liquor movement started around 1981—are at present pushed to the background. Nellore which was not known for any militant movements became the igniting point of anti-liquor women's movement. The CPI(M) which had been concentrating on this question through its science forum called 'Janavignana Vedika' chose to be careful in declaring its identity. While the Nellore movement had succeeded in stopping the liquor auction till today, the Kurnool movement had succeeded in building up village-level resistance in a militant way.

6

GROWING ALCOHOLISM, EXCISE REVENUE AND PUBLIC POLICY

G. Parthasarathy

Mass movements against alcoholism and picketing in front of arrack shops are not new to this country. They had the sanction of Mahatma Gandhi and formed part of his constructive programme during the period of the Nationalist Movement for Independence. The hold of Gandhian thought was so strong on the Constitution makers that prohibition of the consumption of intoxicating drinks and drugs which are injurious to health was madè a directive principle under Article 47 of the Constitution. Yet, the post-independence period has witnessed a drift in public policy relating to prohibition. The revival of the mass movement against arrack shops in recent years by the People's War Group in Telangana followed by a widespread agitation lead by poorer and lower caste women against licensing and sale of liquor necessitate re-examination of public policy. The Andhra Pradesh Government, which has yet to announce its policy decision, appears to be seized with two issues in formulating its policy: firstly, excise is a big revenue yielder and the loss of the revenue needs to be compensated by alternative sources if development tempo needs to be maintained. Secondly, there are issues governing implementation of prohibition, phased versus total prohibition, and possible growth of illicit distillation as a cottage industry. In this event, the objectives of prohibition will be frustrated even while the State revenue gets crippled.

Consumption of Alcohol

There is very little systematic data on the extent of household consumption of alcohol and also its distribution among different social groups. For recent years the NSS is the only source for a country wide analysis. The NSS 43rd Round (1987-88) provides details of number of households consuming alcohol beverages per thousand households statewise by rural and urban areas. These data are based on the response of the households to the question whether the household consumed alcoholic beverages during the month of survey. The data do not provide details on the quantity of consumption but only give an idea of the percentage of households consuming alcoholic beverages.

As per the details provided by NSS, spread of consumption of alcohol beverages was wider in rural areas as compared to the urban. At the All-India level, 14.7 per cent of the rural households reported consumption of alcohol while the corresponding percentage for urban areas was only 10.6 per cent. The incidence of consumption of alcohol as judged by percentage of households consuming, is higher in rural areas at All-India level and also in all States, except Himachal Pradesh, Jammu & Kashmir and Uttar Pradesh.

The State-wise picture shows wide variations in the spread. Andhra Pradesh is one of the States with high spread of consumption of alcohol beverages with 25.3 per cent in rural areas and 16.0 per cent in urban areas. The spread of consumption of alcohol beverages of Andhra Pradesh was only exceeded by Assam in rural areas. Andhra Pradesh ranked high in the spread of consumption of alcoholic beverages in urban areas also (Table 1).

Table 1
State-wise Consumption of Alcoholic Beverages (43rd Round 1987-88) Number Per 1000 Households

	State	*Rural*	*Urban*
1.	Andhra Pradesh	258	160
2.	Assam	259	33
3.	Bihar	174	139
4.	Gujarat	72	35
5.	Haryana	170	146
6.	Himachal Pradesh	191	266
7.	Jammu & Kashmir	50	63
8.	Karnataka	148	125
9.	Kerala	148	112
10.	Madhya Pradesh	224	124
11.	Maharashtra	155	98
12.	Orissa	201	114
13.	Punjab	223	199
14.	Rajasthan	124	106
15.	Tamil Nadu	103	98
16.	Uttar Pradesh	43	45
17.	West Bengal	99	74
	All India	147	106

Source: Sarvekshana, July-September, 1991, pp. 53 & 54.

It appears from NSS data that only one in four in rural areas and one in six in urban areas are given to drinking even in Andhra Pradesh. Considered against popular impression of widespread and growing practice of drinking these figures appear to be under-estimated.

But earlier NSS Studies for Karnataka cited by Simon Musgrave and Nicholas Stern (1985) for 28th Round (1973-74) and for 32nd Round (1977-78) showed that only 9 per cent of the households were given to alcoholic consumption. The ten years following 1977-78, i.e., in 1987-88, showed an appreciable increase in the percentage to 14.00 in Rural Karnataka, suggesting thereby that alcoholism has become more widespread, though households reporting alcoholic consumption continued to form a minority both in rural and in urban areas. It is possible that many given to drinking do not report this to the NSS Investigator. Investigations by individual scholars for around the same years and for the same area showed higher percentages. Thimmaiah and Sharma study (cited by Musgrave and Nicholas Stern, 1985) showed that 28 per cent were given to drinking in Karnataka in 1974-75 as against 9 per cent of the NSS for 1973-74 in Karnataka. A recent study conducted by IDPS in Visakhapatnam city slums in 1991 shows that 47 per cent of the total households in urban slums reported consumption of alcohol.

The following three broad conclusions appear to be justified on the basis of the readily available data:

1. Over time, there has been an increase in the overall percentage of households given to arrack consumption both in rural and urban areas.
2. The incidence of alcohol consumption is quite high in poorer areas like slums even while the overall percentages are low.
3. Percentage of households, consuming alcohol is higher in rural areas as compared to urban, though in urban areas alcoholism should have increased at a rapid rate.

As regards alcohol consumption by social groups, there is very little readily available data for recent years. Data for mid-'70s for Karnataka showed incidence of drinking was higher among households engaged in manual labour as compared to those engaged in non-manual labour. There was a low propensity of consumption of alcohol among non-manual labour groups, especially in the urban areas. The probability of drinking was also found to be higher among SCs and STs.

The NSS, 1987-88, provides data on percentage of households consuming alcohol by per capita expenditure groups. There are no significant variations in the percentage of households reporting consumption among various expenditure groups within rural areas (Table 2). The incidence could still be high among the poorer groups if the frequency and level of intake are high among the poorer households. This might well be the case. As regards urban areas, the percentage of households reporting consumption are high both among the low per capita expenditure groups as well as among the top income groups.

Table 2
Number of Households Reporting per 1000 Households Consumption of Alcoholic Beverages by Monthly per Capita Expenditure Group (Rs.): All-India

Per capita expenditure group	*Rural*	*Urban*
Less than 65	144	98
65 - 80	147	87
80 - 95	150	110
95 - 110	148	109
110 - 125	142	114
125 - 140	143	109
140 - 160	157	92
160 - 180	136	99
180 - 215	149	114
215 - 280	148	91
280 - 385	150	112
Above 385	150	152
	147	106

Source: Sarvekshana, July-September, 1991, p. 471

We also examined the distribution of excise revenue across districts for 1984-85 as presented in the Statistical Abstract of Andhra Pradesh. The per capita excise revenue across the districts in Andhra Pradesh ranged between Rs. 38/- in Medak district to Rs. 109/- in Visakhapatnam District. This is regressed with percentage of urbanisation, percentage of SCs and STs and percentage of households below poverty line. The regression coefficients are not only significant for urbanisation but also for SC and ST proportions at one per cent level suggesting that areas with high concentration of SCs and STs contribute to more excise revenue in per capita terms.

Systematic studies on the impact of alcoholism on the quality of life of the households are not readily available. We press into service the data available in the sample study of urban slums in Visakhapatnam city. Per capita expenditure on food of households reporting alcohol consumption was Rs. 121 per month as against Rs. 129 for those not consuming alcohol. Percentage of children going to school in the age group of 6-14 was found to be 84 per cent as against 88 per cent for those reporting no consumption. The alcoholic household was in deficit budget on the average while the non-alcoholic household showed a surplus of 9.5 per cent on the average. The evidence on differences in general sickness between the two groups is not conclusive. But there are differences in the incidence of chronic diseases; alcoholic households showing higher incidence (See Appendix Tables for Data on Vishakhapatnam Slums).

Following is the sum up of our findings on alcoholism by socio-economic groups and its impact on the quality of life:

1. The incidence of alcoholism is higher among manual labourers.
2. It is higher among the scheduled castes and sched-

uled tribes as compared to other social groups.

3. Alcoholism is positively related to degree of urbanisation and SCs and STs.
4. Households given to alcohol spend less on food, send less proportion of children to school and have more chronically ill persons.
5. The probability of having deficit household budget is more among households given to alcohol, and consequently, their dependence on money lenders could be high; and
6. Poverty alleviation programmes could be frustrated in the context of prevalence of drinking habit.

Excise Revenue

Trends in revenue (Table 3) show that between 1984-85 and 1990-91 there was a doubling of the revenues from State excise. If the budget estimates for 1992-93 are compared with accounts of 1984-85, it would appear that there was a rise of 2.5 times in the excise revenue between 1984-85 and 1992-93. As a share of total tax revenue excise taxes showed an increase over time. What is much more important, a substantial part of excise revenue is got from country spirits which are consumed mainly by the poorer people. In the budget estimates for 1992-93 out of Rs. 862 crores of excise revenue budgeted, Rs. 640 crores or 3/4th are accounted for by the country spirits (Table 4). A substantial part of this is through auction money for licensing trade in arrack. The auction of an arrack shop by the state to the highest bidder is the means by which state over time sought to augment its revenue. The arrack dealer who obtains the lease of right to sell liquor in retail by the highest bid has a stake in promoting arrack consumption. They work for unlimited number of days without holidays. They work for unlimited number of hours from morning till late in the night. Thus, the state which has monopoly of arrack production sought to maximise its revenue by encouraging drinking among the poor groups quite in violation of the fundamental principles. For instance, in Visakhapatnam City, with a population around a million and adult male working population of 300,000, there are 44 toddy shops and 311 arrack shops making a total of 355. Approximately, for every 900 adult male working population there is a shop. Almost all of them are located in residential areas with high concentration in working class areas. As a result of growing dominance of arrack shops, the poor man is induced not only to drink more but is made to shift from the cheaper and less harmful toddy to arrack.

Table 3
Trends in Excise Revenue in Andhra Pradesh

(Rs. in Crores)

	1984-85 (Accounts)	*1985-86 (Revised estimates)*	*1986-87 (Budget estimates)*	*1990-91 (Accounts)*	*1992-93 (Budget estimates)*
State Excise	351.24	405.00	492.00	727.97	862.00
State Taxes	1621.88	1996.79	2314.23	2647.24*	3387.95*
Total Revenue	2293.78	2870.32	3226.88	5347.18	6663.14
Share of Excise in in State Tax	21.66	20.28	21.26	27.50	25.44
Total Receipts...	15.31	14.11	15.25	13.61	12.94

* After exclusion of taxes on income which are got as a share of central excise.

Source: Explanatory Memorandum Part I On the Budget for 1992-93, Government of Andhra Pradesh.

Table 4
Excise Revenue Derived From Arrack

(Rs. in Crores)

	1983-84	1984-85	1985-86	1990-91 accounts	Revised estimates	1992-93 Budgeted estimates
Country Spirits: (arrack)						
(a) Rental on arrack	191.37	221.56	272.73	556.10	600.00	640.00
(b) Duty on arrack	47.98	40.17	43.10			
	239.35	261.73	315.83			
Total Excise Revenue	308.06	328.29	380.66	727.97	784.00	862.40
Share of Country liquor in total excise revenue	77.69	79.72	82.96	76.40	76.53	74.21

Source: Explanatory Memorandum, Part II on the Budget for 1992-93, Government of Andhra Pradesh.

In Andhra Pradesh, the level of excise revenue has been much higher in comparison with All-India. In 1990-91, the share of excise revenue in the total tax revenue of all States at All-India level was 15.8 per cent. In Andhra pradesh, it was 24.4 per cent (Table 5).

Table 5
State Excise Revenue: Andhra Pradesh and All States

(Rs. in Crores)

	All States		*Andhra Pradesh*	
	1990-91 (Accounts)	*1992-93 Budget Estimates*	*1990-91 (Accounts)*	*1992-93 Budget Estimates*
State Excise Duty	4795.0	5959	727.97	862.40
Revenue from State taxes	30347.2	40213	2985.46	3833.94
Share of excise revenue from state excise	15.80	14.82	24.38	22.49

Source: RBI Bulletin, September, 1992.

The Ninth Finance Commission projected the State Excise revenue and the total tax revenue for the period 1990-95 State-wise. The projection showed that in Andhra Pradesh State excise would account for 27.18 per cent of the total tax revenue. Very few states in India exceed this figure (Table 6).

Table 6
State-wise Estimates of Ninth Finance Commission: 1991-95 (Before Finance Commission Transfers)

(Rs. in Crores)

State	*State Excise*	*Tax Revenue*	*The share of State excise in Tax Revenue*
1. Andhra Pradesh	4475.77	16469.51	27.18
2. Assam	63.13	2516.27	2.50
3. Bihar	563.35	6557.24	8.59
4. Gujarat	329.01	13090.54	2.51
5. Haryana	1688.80	6152.43	27.45
6. Himachal Pradesh	277.10	1028.15	26.95

7. Jammu & Kashmir	298.91	1139.92	26.24
8. Karnataka	2571.40	13030.70	19.73
9. Kerala	1218.00	8340.00	14.60
10. Madhya Pradesh	1403.76	8481.97	16.54
11. Maharashtra	3774.40	28418.32	13.28
12. Orissa	267.54	2910.47	9.19
13. Punjab	2591.99	8291.05	31.26
14. Rajasthan	980.27	6499.86	15.08
15. Tamil Nadu	1721.02	17874.75	9.63
16. Uttar Pradesh	2938.95	16031.98	18.27
17. West Bengal	984.27	11653.82	8.44

Source: 2nd Report of the Ninth Finance Commission (for 1991), p. 76.

The burdens of growing State excise revenue are being placed on the poorest section of the society making the structure quite regressive. The tax structure in Andhra Pradesh is more regressive as compared to most of other states as a result of the high share of excise revenue. As in 1990-91, taxes on commodities and services in A.P. accounted for 92 per cent of the total tax revenue, while the corresponding percentage at the level of all states is only 89 per cent.

In brief, the State exercised its monopoly over production and wholesale distribution of arrack, and exploited the propensity to drink of the poorer people in society by extracting maximum revenues from arrack. It showed no concern for the adverse impact of drinking on the budgets of the poor households and on their quality of life. The women's anti-arrack movement is in essence, a movement against the exercise of powers of monopoly of the State over production and wholesale distribution of arrack against the interests of poor violating directive principles and also violating all canons of equity in the tax system.

Issues in Public Policy

One of the major issues in public policy relates to loss of revenue to the tune of Rs. 640 crores through country spirits as per the budget of 1992-93. This is around one-fifth of the total budgeted tax revenue collected by the State. The loss of it needs to be considered against the background of growing deficit of revenue receipts over revenue expenditure (Table 7). As per the budget estimates the deficit was Rs. 218.62 crores in 1992-93. Deficit of State revenue was 6.45 per cent. If the loss of excise tax revenue is not compensated, the deficit is likely to grow much further. The loss of excise revenue should also be considered against the background of increasing payments of interest rates. As per the budget estimates of 1992-93 interest payment of the State Government amounted to Rs. 843 crores. These payments formed around 25 per cent of the tax revenue of the State. The loss of State revenue of excise through prohibition will mean a further rise in debt obligations of the State. The deficit on revenue account for the period 1990-95 as per the Ninth Finance Commission before the Finance Commission transfers, was estimated to be 2,296 crores of rupees. This deficit is likely to grow further. State Government debt as on March 31, 1991 was of the order of Rs. 6,042 crores, of which central loan accounted for Rs. 3,349 crores. This is likely to rise further.

Table 7
Revenue and Expenditure of Andhra Pradesh for Selected Years

(Rs. in Crores)

	1984-85 (Accounts)	*1985-86 (Revised estimates)*	*1986-87 (Budget)*	*1990-91 (Accounts)*	*Revised (Budget estimates)*	*Budget (Estimates)*
Total revenue receipts	2293.78	2870.32	3226.58	5347.18	6072.95	6663.14
Total revenue expenditure	2462.81	2949.58	3242.62	5504.78	6300.11	6881.75
Deficit/ surplus	-169.03	-79.26	-16.04	-157.60	-227.16	-218.61

Source: Explanatory Memorandum, Part-I.

As per the budget of 1992-93, the Central grants and share in taxes as percentage of total revenue amounted to a little more than one third. This dependence on grants and share of the central tax will increase still further in the absence of the excise revenue from arrack.

In brief, the argument is that the ways and means position of the State Government, in the absence of excise revenue, is likely to be much more critical. As a result, tempo on developmental programmes as well as poverty alleviation programmes is likely to slow down as the rate of growth of non-tax revenue is not likely to increase so as to compensate for the fall in growth of tax revenue.

But the preceding arguments are based on the assumption that there is no possibility for fiscal reform and also of economy in expenditure. Such assumptions are not valid and they need to be examined carefully.

Land revenue as per the accounts of 1984-85, was Rs. 17.13 crores. Per hectare land revenue was only Rs. 12. The income per hectare from agriculture in that year was Rs. 2593[1] after making allowances for wages. Agriculturists hardly paid 0.46 per cent of their income from land towards land revenue. Since 1984-85 land revenue increased from Rs. 17 crores to Rs. 29 crores in 1991-92, and as per the budget of 1992-93 it was Rs. 32 crores. Per hectare land revenue rose to Rs. 28; but, as a percentage of agriculturist income, which stood at Rs. 6,500, it was only 0.45 per cent. Top holdings exceeding 7.50 hectares and forming less than 4 per cent whose minimum holding income is around Rs. 50,000, accounted for little more or less than 30 per cent of the total operated area. They contributed to the State revenues only Rs. 358 per holder on the average. While a person at this level of income in the urban areas is liable

1. This is derived by dividing the contribution of agriculture to State domestic product by the total area under operational holdings, and by making downward adjustment for making allowances for wage payment, by agriculturists.

to an income tax of Rs. 7,000. Introduction of agricultural income tax to which only 4 per cent of the holdings would be subjected to, could yield more than Rs. 150 crores, if strictly implemented.

Secondly, the organised sector employees form a privileged class in the State. In March 1991, they numbered 1.73 million out of a total labour force of 28 million or 6 per cent. The public sector accounted for bulk of these workers. The Andhra Pradesh Tax on Profession and Trades and Employees Act 1987 provides for a levy of tax on persons engaged in professions. The rates specified range from Rs. 72 to Rs. 250 per annum. The tax yielded Rs. 27.56 crores in 1991 and the budgeted amount for 1992-93 was Rs. 30.39 crores. Following the example of tax on urban people for supporting employment guarantee scheme in Maharashtra, there has been a justification for imposing additional tax rate on this privileged class. The tax rate could be doubled and this could yield in addition of Rs. 32 crores which could be specifically assigned to the local bodies for rehabilitation of arrack addicts especially in the urban areas.

We could also expect an addition to the revenue from sales tax even if there were no rise in the rates of sales tax. However, the total sales tax levied on commodities commonly consumed by the poor as in 1984-85 was estimated to be only Rs. 74 crores out of Rs. 607 crores or 11.64 per cent. If the arrack consumption is assumed to be 15 per cent of the total budget of the poorer households, there would be a release of 15 per cent for expenditure on items commonly consumed by them. The sales tax levied on the commodities commonly consumed by the poorer section of the people would be of the order of Rs. 227 crores out of the total sales tax revenue of Rs. 1669 crores as in 1992-93 budget. We could expect a rise of 10 per cent in food expenditure of the arrack drinkers as a result of 15 per cent rise in expenditure, assuming an elasticity of 0.67. Consequently, we could expect a rise of 10 per cent in the sales tax levied on the commodities additionally consumed by the poor. The sales tax additions could be estimated to be Rs. 23 crores.

Entertainment tax as in 1990-91, yielded Rs. 38 crores, and as per the budget of 1992-93 Rs. 46.73 crores. If a third of this is assumed to be paid by the poorer groups, it amounts to around Rs. 15 crores. If elasticity of entertainment expenditure is assumed to be unity a 15 per cent rise in expenditure would yield a 15 per cent rise in entertainment tax. This would yield another Rs. 2 crores as a result of prohibition.

The possibilities for augmenting revenue by raising user charges on economic and social services are great. It is estimated (Sudipto Mundle and Govinda Rao, May 4, 1991) that the total cost of social and economic services as in 1987-88 for Andhra Pradesh was Rs. 2,737 crores. Out of this only Rs. 447.43 crores or 16.35 per cent were recovered and Rs. 2,289.33 crores formed the subsidy (Table 8). The benefits of the subsidies accrued to a small proportion of population using the services. As a consequence of this, there are a small and relatively privileged section of the population who gets these services virtually free and hence appropriate a large consumer surplus while the vast majority did not have access to these services let alone availing subsidies (Mundle & Govinda Rao, p. 1163). Recovery rates on Higher and Technical Education, which are received only by a small section of the people were as low as 1.37 per cent and 2.71 per cent respectively. As regards, economic services, irrigation and power along with road transport constituted three important services accounting for low recovery rate. The recovery rate on economic services is hardly 30.00 per cent. Even in public enterprises the recovery rate is hardly one third.

Table 8
Subsidies in Andhra Pradesh as In 1987-88

Social & Economic Services	*Rs. in Crores*	%
Education	675.72	29.52
Medical and Public Health	222.78	9.73
Water Supply, Sanitation and Housing	165.55	7.23
Other Social Services	252.09	11.01
Total Social Services	**1316.14**	**57.49**
Agriculture and allied services	529.18	23.12
Irrigation	354.54	15.49
Power and Electricity	28.18	1.24
Industry and Mineral	47.21	2.06
Transport and Communication	89.97	3.93
Total Economic Services	**973.19**	**42.51**
Total Subsidy	2289.33	10.00

Source: E.P.W., May 4, 1991, pp. 1166 & 1168

It is not difficult to raise alternative resources to compensate for the loss of excise revenue, provided there is a political will. In the budget 1992-93 revenue expenditure on social and economic services accounted for Rs. 4,789 crores. Revenue receipts on account of these items are hardly Rs. 329 crores. Even if one-fifth of the expenditure is recovered, it is possible to compensate for the losses from prohibition of arrack. Proper pricing of services like higher education, irrigation or electricity, would not only help in raising larger revenues but also would result in the more economic use of resources. The vulnerable sections or the target groups can be helped through selective subsidies (Govinda Rao, 1992). Improvement of performance of power utilities could gain more revenues. The poor performance of these has been due to a variety of reasons. The important of these are: poor operating efficiency, lop-sided tariff structure particularly charging very low rates for agricultural consumption; high transmission and distribution losses; huge arrears in revenue collection; and inordinate delays in construction and commissioning of power projects. In Andhra Pradesh price charged for supplying power for agricultural consumption was 4.5 paise while the operating cost was 64.3 paise per k.w.h. (Govinda Rao, 1992).

There must also be a careful review of all centrally sponsored schemes for their leakages.

In brief, the issue of alternative sources of revenue is resolvable. In fact, tax is a shift of resources from private to public use. And it is justifiable only if it contributes to equity and also to more efficient use of resources. Revenue from arrack is the most inequitable tax. It does not satisfy the canons of taxation. It affects adversely the quality of life of people, which the State seeks to promote through its expenditure. In such a context the consideration of alternative sources could be considered even irrelevant.

One of the most important issue is implementation. Firstly, if arrack alone is prohibited, and not toddy and other types of liquor, the arrack drinkers may shift to others. But prohibition of other types of liquor raises complex issues. But we will need a policy which will prevent labour class shifting from arrack to expensive liquor. The drinkers of foreign liquor in particular generally belong to a class of educated, and relatively affluent group. Most of them could be expected to drink discriminatingly, and for entertainment. Excise tax on them is an easy means of raising revenue. While there is need for regulation even in this case, prohibition may not be necessary.

Even a more difficult issue is illicit distillation. Both the US experience and the experience of Gujarat, a state in which there is prohibition are worth recalling. In 1919, the anti-saloon league pushed through the 18th amendment in the

U.S. Constitution (Repealed in 1933). National prohibition law and nearly 200,000 saloons were destroyed. Consumption fell in the early years of prohibition, especially among the poor. But moonshining and smuggling gave drinking break to the middle and upper classes, brought the mob into the business and prompted a path of blindness and deaths from drinking wood alcohol. (National Geographical Magazine, Feb. 1992, p. 11, Alcohol, The Legal Drug by Boyd Gibbons). Evidence before the Tek Chand Committee (1964) also brings out wide prevalence of illicit distillation in Gujarat.

Prohibition in the absence of mass movement by women may lead to a situation of widespread illicit distillation. Mass movement without Government's firm commitment to prohibition can not be sustained as women get harassed by a overzealous police acting in the interests of arrack bosses, and claiming to protect public order. Mass movement against arrack gains a legal status in the context of prohibition. As a prelude to prohibition of arrack, its selling should be immediately regulated by the State. Such a regulation is warranted by the Directive Principles of the State Policy enumerated by the Constitution. It is morally justifiable. Moreover, political sagacity would require sensitivity to the women's movement. The number of licensed shops should be restricted. These should not operate in residential areas. They should work only during pre-set hours. They should not work on pay days and also on festival days. The alcohol content should be reduced to the minimum. All these must come into force immediately. A target date needs to be set for total prohibition of arrack, with programmes of rehabilitation and recreation for addicts. The women's movements should continue for a decade to come and should be geared to the needs of preventing illicit distillation on the model of Nashabandi Mandal of Gujarat State. If eternal vigilance is the price of liberty, the best safeguard against the evil of drinking is women power. It is the minimum obligation of the State to ensure that such a healthy movement is not obstructed or thwarted.

REFERENCES

Govt. of Andhra Pradesh, *Explanatory Memorandum*, Part I on the Budget for 1992-93.

Govt. of Andhra Pradesh, *Explanatory Memorandum*, Part II on the Budget for 1992-93.

Second Report of the Ninth Finance Commission for 1990-95.

Mundle Sundipto and Rao Govinda, '*Volume and Composition of Government Subsidies*', *Economic and Political Weekly*, May 4, 1991.

Govindarao, M., *State Level Budgetary Reforms*, Indian Economic Association Trust for Research and Development, 1992.

Statistical Abstract of Andhra Pradesh, 1985-86.

Gibbons Byod, "Alcohol, the Legal Drug," National Geographical Magazine, Feb. 1992.

Planning Commission, Government of India, *Report of the Prohibition Enquiry Committee*, vol. 2, 1965.

Simon Musgrave and Nicholas Stern, *Alcohol: Demand and Taxation in South India in the 1970s*, University of Warwick, Jan. 1985.

Government of Andhra Pradesh, *Survey of Economic Trends and State Plan*, 1992-93.

Appendix 1
Arrack Consumers Compared to Non-Arrack Consumers in the Slums of Visakhapatnam City—1990-91

	Consuming Arrack	*Not Consuming Arrack*	*Total*
Households Sample	285	327	612
Percentage Consuming	46.57	53.43	100.00
Percapita Expenditure on Arrack per month (in Rs.)	37.00	—	18.00
Percapita total expenditure on all items per month (in Rs.)	243.00	218.00	230.00
Percapita income (in Rs.)	228.00	241.00	235.00
Percentage of alcohol expenditure in total cosnumption	15.23	—	7.83
Percentage of children (6-14 years) going to School	83.73	87.68	85.89
Percapita expenditure on food per month	121.00	129.00	125.00
Percentage deficit/surplus of income over expenditure	-6.58	+9.54	2.13

Source: Data Sheets of Evaluation Study of Visakhapatnam Slum Improvement Project, IDPS, 1991.

Appendix 2
Distribution of Alcoholics and Non-Alcoholics Within Each Caste Group: Vishakhapatnam Slums—1991

Caste	*Alcoholics*	*Non-Alcoholics*	*Total*
Forward Caste	35.42	64.58	100.00
Backward Class	46.56	53.44	100.00
Scheduled Caste	51.15	48.85	100.00
Scheduled Tribe	66.67	33.33	100.00
Others	33.33	66.67	100.00
Total	46.57	53.43	100.00

Source: Data Sheets of Evaluation Study, IDPS, 1991.

Appendix 2(A)
Percentage of Alcoholic and Non-Alcoholic Within Income Group: Visakhapatnam Slums—1991

Income Group	*Alcoholic*		*Non-Alcoholic*		*Total*	
	No.	*%*	*No.*	*%*	*No.*	*%*
Below Rs. 1000	155	47.84	169	52.16	324	100.00
Above Rs. 1000	130	45.14	158	54.86	288	100.00
	285	46.56	327	53.44	612	100.00

Source: Data Sheets, IDPS.

Appendix 3
Distribution of Chronic Diseased Persons in the Sample Households (6-12): Vishakhapatnam Slums—1991

	Alcoholic Households	*Non-Alcoholic Households*
Total Population	1391	1498
No. reporting chronic diseases	51	44
% in total population of the respective categories	3.67	2.74

Source: Data Sheets, IDPS.

Appendix 4
Distribution of Gainfully Occupied by Alcoholic and Non-alcoholic Within Each Occupation Group: Vishakhapatnam Slums: 1991

Type of Occupation	*Alcoholic*	*Non-Alcoholic*	*Total*
Unskilled labourers	58.33	41.67	100.00
Skilled labourers	42.64	57.36	100.00
Service Occupations	39.82	60.18	100.00
Trade/petty establishments/ restaurants, etc.	47.50	52.50	100.00
Office jobs and professions	37.25	62.75	100.00
Pensioners	36.00	64.00	100.00
Total	50.28	49.72	100.00

Source: IDPS, data sheets.

Appendix 5
Consumption of Country Spirits

Year	*Country spirit (in lakh bulk litres)*	*Index*
1979-80	670.55	100
1980-81	697.44	104
1981-82	696.11	104
1982-83	741.31	111
1983-84	841.82	125
1984-85	864.18	129
1985-86	887.00	132
1991-92 (approximate)	1112.00	166

Value of arrack sold as in 1990-91 (in crores of Rs.) = 1112
Value of arrack sold as a percentage of State Domestic Product = 3.97
Value of liquor sold as a percentage of estimate income = 15.0.

Section-II

ALCOHOLISM AND ETHICAL ISSUES

7

CONSUMPTION OF ALCOHOL, ETHICAL ISSUES AND PROHIBITION

—R. Venkata Rao

The Liquor Evil From A to Z

Arms more villains,
Breaks more laws,
Corrupts more officials,
Destroys more homes,
Engulfs more fortunes,
Fills more jails,
Grows more gray hairs,
Harrows more hearts,
Incites more crime,
Jeopardises more lives,
Kindles more strife,
Lacerates more feelings,
Maims more bodies,
Nails down more coffins,
Opens more graves,
Places more feet on the downward path,
Quenches more hopes,
Raises more sobs,
Sells more virtues,
Tells more lies,
Undermines more youth,
Valids more contracts,
Wrecks more men,

Xcites more murders,
Yields more disgrace,
Zeros more hopes.

Ever since the first man got drunk there has been a debate with equal vehemance on either side of prohibition. If a teetotaller and great thinker like Betrand Russel denotes drunkenness as "temporary suicide" and the happiness it brings as "negative and momentary," an equally distinguished and successful person like Winston Churchill claimed "I have taken more out of alcohol than alcohol has taken out of me." It is said that if a Puritan asks "What key will unlock the door to hell?" and he himself answers, he would say `whiskey,' while many eminent personalities like Byron, Keats and Shelly assured that alcohol opens the portals of paradise. The question is who is right?

"The prohibition law is written for weaklings and derelicts" wrote Mrs. Sabin in 1931. It has divided the nation into three parts Wets, Drys and Hypocrites. This is as true to India as any other country.

Much can be said on both the sides. In fact, in India neither drinking nor abstinence is traditional. If one glances through the pages of the history, one could observe that if some rulers were wine bibbers, some others were puritanical prohibitionists. By and large the rich and the poor consumed liquor, the middle class did not. Excepting for rare occasions the State left the question of drinking to the citizen to decide for himself. This continued from ancient times down to the British. It was under the influence of Mahatma Gandhi that in 1937 at the Madras Session, the Indian National Congress adopted a resolution on prohibition as a part of its programme. The party accepted it because it was a potential and powerful weapon against imported liquor, and it should be observed that only a small majority of Gandhians supported it on moral grounds. Prohibition became an essential part of the Bill of Rights adopted by the Karachi Session. After independence it was incorporated into the Constitution as a Directive Principle of State Policy. In the meantime, in a number of states prohibition was tried with varying degrees of efficacy. After 1947, Andhra Pradesh, Bombay, Madras and Saurashtra went totally dry for sometime. An interesting observation is that prohibition was successful where the majority of the people were in any case non-drinkers and it failed where people such as Adivasis and Martial races like Rajputs and Gurkhas were habituated to drinking.

Notwithstanding, the ethical discussion about wisdom of imposing prohibition, it must never be forgotten that the problem of drinking which leads to drunkenness, has been assuming menacing proportions in recent times. Particularly, adolescents are becoming more and more vulnerable to this evil practice. It is not surprising that indiscriminate opening of wine shops within the striking distances of Educational Institutions and the official patronising of Abkari have in no less way contributed to the menace.

One can not but admit that the impact of drinking can be disastrous on the individual, the family, the society and the State. In India, drinking was frowned upon and was punishable in Vedic and pre-vedic period. The puranas condemned the use of wine and there are references in Sutras. 'Manusmriti' considered drinking of sura among the five mortal sins, meriting severest punishment. Book-XI of Manusmriti says "Sura is of three kinds made from jaggery, grains and Mahua flowers, respectively known as Gaudi, Paishty, and Madhri." It is forbidden to drink these beverages.

Sura and flesh are the food of Rakshasas and Pisachas and a person who offers prayers to God must not take such substances. The pure man stupefied by drunkenness might fall on something impure or improperly pronounce vedic text or commit some other act which ought not to be committed.

The man who drinks sura and man who violates a Guru's bed, must be considered as men who committed

Mahapataka (mortal sins). Manu considered drinking by women as the cause of their ruin. He said "drinking sura, associating with wicked people, separation from husband, rambling abroad, sleeping at unseasonable hours, and dwelling in other mens houses are the six causes for the ruination of women. She who drinks liquor is of bad conduct, rebellious, diseased, mischievous and wasteful.

Sura, indeed is the dirty refuse of grain and therefore, a person shall not drink Sura. Manu's abhorrence was also shared to an equal degree by the famous law giver Yagna Valkya. He prescribed penance which amounted to self destruction.

Even Archbishop Francis De S Feneloen (1651-1715) observes "some of the most dreadful mischiefs proceed from wine; it is the cause of disease, quarrels, sedition, idleness, aversion to labour, and every species of domestic disorder."

As far as India is concerned, the case for prohibition is very strong. Bringing prohibition slowly and piece-meal will not yield results. Such an experiment would fail so that it would be said that prohibition could never be tried or that it could never be successful. Mahatma Gandhi said "you will try to do the right thing in the wrong manner and then denounce the right thing instead of the wrong manner... The country is in favour of prohibition. If it is a question of lakhs and lakhs of signatures in favour of prohibition it is merely a matter of organisation. I have not found a single place where there has been real agitation against prohibition except from its manufacturers and financiers. There are states where territorial prohibition has been declared and where not a single man has come forward to say "we want a shop atleast here." Mahatma Gandhi wanted people not to fall into the financial trap. He said "if you are a fierce prohibitionist like myself and if you will agitate from one end of the country to the other for prohibition, you will certainly succeed. Let us not fall into the financial trap that is laid for us. Our position should be absolutely clear. It is not our purpose to find the finances.

Those who committed initial blunder must retrace their steps. The experience of countries which had tried prohibition is that the people have become better and that no financial crisis will befall if prohibition is introduced in india. It is the solemn duty of everyone of us to see the use of drink wiped out of the Land altogether if we possibly can. If I had the power and if I could have my way, I would do so today."

The loss of revenue is only apparent. Removal of this degrading tax through prohibition enables the drinker to earn and spend better. Therefore, apart from the moral and social gain it means a substantial economic gain to the nation. Excise makes people pay their own corruption, moral, mental and physical.

One cannot draw prohibition programme in a proper Bania-spirit. One wonders what will be the so called revenue personnel do if all the wine-bibbers suddenly give up drink. They will manage somehow, it may be answered. Why will they not do so voluntarily? Surely, merit lies in doing the right thing voluntarily not compulsorily.

It has been wrongly suggested that prohibition is an undue interference with the liberty of the individual. It is argued that those who wish to drink must have facilities provided for them. Does it mean that the State should cater for vices of its people. No State regulates or licences houses of ill-fame. No one would provide facilities for thieves in their propensity for thieving.

As there can be no liberty for one to steal, there can be no liberty to sell liquor. Liberty and licence are not the same thing.

It is trite that thieving will continue till Doomsday. Must it, therefore, be licensed? Is thieving of the mind less criminal than thieving of matters? Illicit distillation to an extent will no doubt go on? Its quantity will be the measure of the Government's effort assisted by a vigilant public in the shape of continuous and sympathetic treatment of the drinkers. Moral elevation demands a price no less than material or physical elevation. Our freedom will be the freedom of slaves if we continue to be the victims of drink. Is any cost too much to establish prohibition in all the States? If prohibition is to be a great moral awakening in India the closing of liquor shops should be the indispensable beginning of the moment ending in the complete weaning from drink of the poor people as well as the rich people.

What is needed today is a role model worthy of emulation. Unfortunately, these role models are fast vanishing, if not non-existing, from our public life.

8

INTOXICATING LIQUORS
Vis-a-Vis
REGULATORY MEASURES UNDER THE CONSTITUTION

—*Y. Satyanarayana*

The preamble to the Indian Constitution sets out aims and aspirations of the people of India and these have been translated into the various provisions of the Constitution. The objectives before the Constituent Assembly were to constitute India into a Sovereign Democratic Republic and to secure to its citizen's justice, liberty, equality and fraternity. The ultimate aim of the makers of the Constitution was to have a welfare state and an egalitarian society projecting the aims and aspirations of the people of India who made the extreme sacrifice for attainment of the country's freedom.

Part-IV of the Indian Constitution enumerates certain Directive Principles of the State Policy which are declared as fundamental in the governance of the country. These principles are intended to be the imperative basis of state policy. They are really in the nature of instructions issued to future legislatures and executive for their guidance. Underlying the need of the Directive Principles of the State Policy, Dr. Ambedkar, Chairman of the drafting committee of the Indian Constitution said:

The directive principles are like the Instrument of Instructions which were issued to the Governor-General and to the Governors of the colonies and to those of India by the

British Government under the Act of 1935. The only difference is that they are instructions to the Legislature and the Executive. Such a thing is to my mind to be welcomed wherever there is a grant of power in general terms for peace, order and good government. It is necessary that it should be accompanied by instructions regulating its exercise.

Directive Principles of the State Policy differ in one vital respect from the Fundamental Rights incorporated in the Constitution. Whereas the former are non-justiciable rights, the latter are justifiable rights. They have expressly been excluded from the purview of the courts. This want of enforceability had led a critic to describe them as "a little more than a manifesto of aims and aspirations." The criticism is, however, unjustified as these are only directives and not justiciable rights. This is so because the directive principles require positive action on the part of the state, and, therefore, can be guaranteed only so far as practicable. They are not like the Fundamental Rights which speak of certain things which the State ought to refrain from doing. The authorities of the State may not have to answer for the breach in a law court, but they will certainly have to answer for them to the electorate at election time. These principles have great educational value. They are really in the nature of moral/precepts for the authorities of the State.

Directive Principles and Fundamental Rights together constitute the core of the constitution and represent the basic rights inherent in human beings in this country. There is no inherent conflict between the Directive Principles and Fundamental Rights and both are equally relevant in promoting the aims and objectives of the constitution. However, in translating them into socio-economic reality some degree of compromise is inevitable. Indian Constitution is founded on the bedrock of the balance between the Directive Principles and Fundamental Rights and to tilt the balance by giving supremacy to one over the another is to destroy the harmony of the constitution which is one of the basic features of the constitution.

Among the economic rights and the principles of social security which the state is required to ensure to the people are, raising the level of nutrition; and improvement of public health.

Since the time of the French Revolution, there has been a growing awareness of the close link between political freedom and social justice. It is felt that content of political freedom can be impaired by the absence of social justice. Unless there was adequate protection of social and economic rights, classical individual liberties like the right to equality, liberty of person and freedom of speech might lose much of their significance and even face a serious threat for their own survival. The aftermath of the First World War also highlighted the fact that peace in the World can be established only if it is based on social justice. A number of modern constitutions accordingly embodied within themselves declarations of principles which emphasise the duty of the state to strive for social security and to provide work, education and proper conditions of employment for the citizens. Most of these social and economic rights are of such a nature that it is not considered feasible to provide for their enforcement through the machinery of courts. The Constitutional declarations are more or less in the nature of a pledge on the part of the State that it would strive for attainment of the objectives visualised in the principles. In this context, I am reminded of the Declaration of the Rights of Man of 1793 which states thus:

In order that this declaration, being ever present to all the members of the social body, may unceasingly remind them of their rights and duties; in order that the acts of the legislative power and those of the executive power may be at each moment compared with the aim of every political institution and thereby may be more respected; and in order that the demands of the citizens, grounded henceforth upon simple and untestable principle, may always take the direction of maintaining the constitution and welfare of all.

The Indian National Congress in its Resolution passed in 1931 declared that "in order to end the exploitation of masses, political freedom must include real economic freedom of the starving millions, and that the organisation of economic life must conform to the principle of justice."

The subject of fundamental rights figured prominently in the deliberations of the Sapru Committee appointed by the All Party Conference during the year 1944-45. Subsequently, the British Cabinet Mission Plan 1946 envisaged the setting-up of an Advisory Committee for reporting, *inter alia*, on Fundamental Rights. It was however, in the objectives of Resolution adopted on January 22, 1947, that the Constituent Assembly solemnly pledged itself to draft, for India's future governance a constitution wherein "shall be guaranteed and secured to all the people of India justice, social, economic and political, equality of status, of opportunity and before the law: freedom of thought, expression, belief, faith, worship, vocation, association and action, subject to law and morality."

It is proper to mention here the Fundamental Rights guaranteed under Article 19(1) (g) and 21, and interpret their content and scope in the light of Article 47 of the Constitution as one of the Directive Principles of State Policy. The Supreme Court interpreting the scope of Articles 19(1) (g), 47 and Entry 8 of List II in the VII Schedule held that "the state has exclusive right or privilege or manufacturing and selling liquor. The State grants such right or privilege in the shape of licence or a lease. The State has the power to hold a public auction for grant of such right or privilege and accept payment of a sum in consideration for grant of lease."

Entry 8 of List II of the Constitution empowers the State government to legislate with regard to intoxicating liquor, that is to say, production, manufacture, possession, transport, purchase and sale of intoxicating liquor. One of the purposes of regulation is to raise revenue. There is no Fundamental Right of citizens to carry on trade or do business in liquor. There is the police power of the State to enforce public morality to prohibit trades in noxious or dangerous goods. There is power of the State to enforce an absolute prohibition of manufacture or sale of intoxicating liquor. Article 47 states that the State shall endeavour to bring about prohibition or the consumption except for medicinal purposes of intoxicating drinks and of drugs which are injurious to health. The history of excise law shows that the State has the exclusive right or privilege of manufacture or sale of liquor. Trade in liquor has historically stood on a different footing from other trades. Restrictions which are not permissible in other trades are lawful and reasonable as far as the trade in liquor is concerned. That is why even prohibition of the trade in liquor is not only permissible but also reasonable. The reasons are, public morality, public interest and harmful and dangerous character of the liquor.

In P. N. Kaushal V. Union of India, the Supreme Court was again faced with the question of right to carry on trade or business in liquor, and it held that the right is subject to State's power. It observed that assuming that the petitioner had a Fundamental Right to carry on trade or business in intoxicants, the State certainly has the power to trade or business vis-a-vis unreasonableness, arbitrariness and vacuum of indicium for that exercise. These observations reopen the question whether a citizen can claim a Fundamental Right to liquor.

In Crowley V.Christensen it was held that "there is no inherent right in a citizen to sell intoxication liquor by retail, it is not a privilege of a citizen of the state or of a citizen of the United States. It is business attended with danger to the community. It may, as already said, be entirely prohibited, or be permitted under such conditions as will limit to the utmost its evil. The manner and extent of regulation rests in the discretion of the governing authority." In Bharucha's case the Supreme Court concurred with the observations in Crowley V. Christensen.

In State of Bombay V. F. N. Balsara the Supreme Court referred to Article 47 and said that the idea of prohibition was connected with public health. Challenge to prohibition law under Articles 14 and 19 was repealed on the grounds of public health. The court held that absolute prohibition of manufacture or sale of liquor is permissible and only exception can be for medicinal preparations. The concept of inherent right of citizens to do business in liquor is antithetical to the power of the State to enforce prohibition laws in respect of liquor. The Constitution Bench of the Apex Court in Amar Chandra Chakraborty V. Collector of Excise Department of Government of Tripura held that trade or business in country liquor has from its inherent nature being treated by the State and the society as a special category requiring legislative control. This trade or business is treated as a class by itself and cannot be treated on the same basis as other trades while considering Article 14.

It is pertinent here to discuss briefly the content and scope of "the right to life and personal liberty" guaranteed under Art. 21 of the Constitution. It states that no person shall be deprived of his life or personal liberty except according to the procedure established by law. The `right of life,' is the most fundamental of all. In an American case, it was held that by the term `life' something more is meant than mere animal existence. The inhibition against its deprivation extends to all those limbs and faculties by which life is enjoyed. The expression `liberty' observed the US Supreme Court, is not confined to mere bodily restraint, and `liberty' under law, extends to the full range of conduct which the individual is free to pursue.

Under the State monopoly intoxicating liquor is available in abundance at exorbitant rates. Under the guise of regulation the State has entrusted this noxious trade entirely to the private traders. Noxious goods whether traded by the State itself or by private persons will have the same dangerous character, endangering the life and liberty of those who consume them. For the purpose of revenue the State monopolised trade in intoxicating liquor and is earning at the cost of life, liberty, family relations and economic conditions of millions of citizens living below poverty line. The State has power to regulate the freedoms guaranteed to citizens under Art, 19, but who can regulate the freedom of State in monopolising certain noxious trades, which are not guaranteed to it under the Constitution? From time immemorial, the evil of liquor trade is shadowing the society, severely affecting public health.

The negative mandate contained in Art. 21 against the State is violated by the State in monopolising noxious trades affecting public health, consequently infringing upon the right to life and liberty of those whom the State is meant to represent.

Section-III

HEALTH ASPECTS AND DE-ADDICTION OF ALCOHOLICS

9

PHYSICAL AND PSYCHIATRIC ASPECTS OF ALCOHOLISM

—Dr. P. Ramakrishna

Introduction

Wine is perhaps one of the oldest known alcoholic beverage which traces its antiquity to atleast 5000 BC. Ancient Greece, Rome and the Near East knew the drink well. The Old Testament refers to wine and sacrifice its use in the mass, baptism and other formal ceremonies. Rig-vedic India had known and used two drinks—"Soma" and "Sura."

"Sura" was more likely a fermented wine and probably had a high alcohol content, its high potency invited disapproving remarks from priestly poets. While "Soma" was associated with religious rites, "Sura" was secular and probably drunk just for pleasure. "Chang," the rice brew of Nepal and the Terai region, is closer to the wines of other countries and cultures and considered good for health. "Sake," the wine of Japan has enjoyed a similar health seal of approval.

In many circles of society, alcohol has become the symbol of prestige and the quantity consumed has become the symbol of manliness, strength, and endurance. Alcohol is served freely at most of the celebrations of the affluent class.

In lower classes, the daily wage earner of labour class spends most of his income in drinking, in the firm belief that it is essential for relaxation and sleep. As one witnesses the steady increase in pubs and bars in various cities, it seems certain that the magnitude of abuse of alcohol is rising. The alarming increase in the proportion of young people with serious alcoholic problems brings home the urgent need for effective preventive methods.

Alcoholism remains a major cause of medical, psychiatric, social and economic morbidity. Alcohol abuse adversely affects virtually all systems in the body and is a leading cause of accident-related deaths. After heart disease and cancer, alcoholism is the third largest health problem. Alcohol is the major psycho-active drug used worldwide. Alcoholism is one of the major causes of admission to mental health centres and general hospitals.

Definition

According to D.S.M.III-R, Alcohol dependence is characterised by anyone of the following three major patterns of Pathological alcohol use-

(i) the need for daily use of large amounts of alcohol for adequate functioning;

(ii) regular heavy drinking limited to week ends; and,

(iii) long periods of sobriety interspersed with binges of heavy alcohol intake lasting for weeks or months.

The above patterns are associated with the following behaviour:

(a) Inability to cutdown or stop drinking;

(b) Repeated efforts to control or reduce excessive drinking (periods of temporary abstinence);

(c) Binges (remaining intoxicated throughout the day for atleast two days);

(d) Occasional consumption of a fifth of spirits;

(e) Amnesty periods of events occurring while intoxicated (blackouts);

(f) Continuation of drinking despite serious physical disorder;

(g) Drinking non-beverage alcohol.

Alcoholics show impaired social and occupational functioning, violence, absence from job or legal difficulties. Approximately 13 per cent of all adults suffer from alcoholisms. The onset of alcoholism generally takes place later in women than in men. Alcoholism reduces life expectancy by 10 years.

Etiology

1. *Genetic Factor*: There is a strong genetic factor in the development of alcoholism. Children of alcoholic parents become alcoholic about 4 times more often than the children of non-alcoholic parents; sons of alcoholic parents are more likely to become alcoholic than daughters.

2. *Phychoanalytical Factors*: Persons with harsh, superegos who are self-punitive turn to alcohol as a way of diminishing unconscious stress. The alcoholic personality is described as shy, isolated, impatient, irritable, anxious, hypersensitive and sexually repressed.

3. *Cultural Factors*: Some cultures are more restrained than others about alcohol consumption. It is a custom in some of the communities to serve alcohol and consume in groups in ceremonies, functions, etc.

4. *Learning Theory*: Learning theory suggests that alcohol results in a temporary reduction of fear and conflict which strengthens the drive to drink. The release of anxiety arising from the first drinking experience is the source of reinforcement in alcohol dependence.

5. *Biological Factors*: Recently it has been demonstrated that ethanol may have much more specific effects on selected neurotransmitter systems, particularly the GABA SYSTEM. This finding helps to explain the cross tolerance

and addictive effects that can occur where alcohol is used in combination with barbiturates and benzodaizpines, both of which also act on the GABA system. Ethanol also has effects on non-adrenergic neurons of the ventral tegmental area. Dopamin is believed to be a messenger in brain areas that mediate some of the feelings induced by alcohol that lead to its repeated use. Recent research into hereditary mechanisms in alcoholism has suggested an association between the alcoholism and the gene for a sub-type of dopamin (binding protein). However, the nature of association remains controversial. Preliminary studies indicate that alcoholics are born with faulty liver enzyme system that may lead to their addiction which indicates that alcoholics do not metabolize alcohol normally.

6. *Agent Factors*: Availability, cost, laws and regulation; Pharmacological: High Euphoria (P.R.F.); Tolerance; Conditional withdrawal (S.R.R.)

7. *Environmental:* Cultural, family influence, peer-group interaction. Acceptance of chemical "Coping Mechanism," decreased religiosity; increased secularism; alienation from society; poverty; affluence.

8. *Psychological Factors*: Curiosity: rebelliousness; anti-social personality, depressed mood, low academic performance, social phobia, low frustration tolerance, low self esteem, impulsivity.

9. *Global Factors*: Degree of freedom; Value system of society; Promotion of drug with life in T.V. and Radio; Interest of Government (Revenue).

Effects of Alcohol

Alcohol is absorbed from the ailmentary tract and carried by the blood to the brain and other organs of the body. Alcohol is metabolized in the liver by alcohol dehydrogenase (ADH) and Aldehyde dehydrogenase (Ald. DH). The speed with which alcohol enters the blood stream depends mainly on the following factors:

(i) the amount and type of food in the stomach,

(ii) the type of beverage consumed and its alcohol concentration,

(iii) the circumstances under which it is being drunk,

(iv) drinker's constitutional state.

The intoxicating effects are greater when the blood alcohol concentration is rising than when it is falling (the Mellanby effect).

At a level of 0.05 per cent alcohol in blood, thought, judgement and restraint are disturbed. At a concentration of 0.10 per cent, voluntary motor activity becomes clumsy. The legal intoxication ranges from 0.10 to 0.15 per cent blood alcohol level. At 0.20 per cent, the functions of the entire motor area of the brain is depressed. At 0.30 per cent the person becomes confused or trapped into stupor. At 0.40 to 0.50 per cent, a person is in a coma.

At higher levels, the person may die due to respiratory depression or aspiration of vomitus.

The alcohol content in some of the alcoholic beverages are given as follows:

Whisky Brandy Arrack Rum 40-55%	Wines 10-20%	Beer Toddy 6-8%
by vol.	by vol.	by vol.
30 ML (1 drink) (1 OZ)	60 ML (1 drink) (2 OZ)	285 ML (1 drink) (10 OZ)

Hazards of Long Term use of Alcohol

1. G.I.T.	-	Oesophagitis; Gastritis, Acholorhydria, Ulcers, Chronic Pancreatitis, Hepatitis, Cirrhosis of Liver.
2. C.V.S.	-	Munich Beer Heart-Cardio Myopathy, Hypertension, Coronary Heart Disease
3. R.S.	-	Aspiration Pneumonia, Lung Abscess, T.B.
4. Immune System	-	Impairs cellular immunity with delayed Hypersensitivity
5. Metabolism	-	Water-Electrolyte imbalance
6. Skeletal	-	Alcoholic Myopathy
7. Reproductive System	-	Testicular Atrophy: Loss of Libido Fetal Alcohol Syndrome
8. C.N.S.	-	Polyneuropathy; Cerebeller Degeneration; Amblyopia; Seizures; Korsakoff's Syndrome; Wernicke's Encephalopathy
9. Effects Eye	-	Nutritional Blindness; Cataract; Iridicyclitis; Secondary Glaucoma; Complicated cataract; Macular Degeneration; Retinopathy; Alcoholic Optic Atrophy.
10. Organic Mental Disorders	-	Personality Changes; Pschosis; Alcohol Intoxication; Alcohol withdrawal Delirium (Delirium tremens) Alcohol Hallucinosis; Dementia; Fetal Alcohol Syndrome.

DELIRIUM TREATMENTS (D.Ts):

Features

D.Ts occurs within one week after the person stops drinking or reduces his intake—Autonomic hyperactivity (Tachycardia, Sweating, increased B.P.) disorientation and clouding of consciousness; Perceptual disturbances; (visual or tactile hellucinations) Hyper excitability to lethargy; Delusions and agitated behaviour, Fever, Seizers. D.Ts has mortality rate of 20 per cent. Death is due to intercurrent medical illnesses such as: Pneumonia; Renal Disease; Hepatic Insufficiency or Heart Failure.

Treatment

(a) Benzodiazepine 25-50 mg of Chlordiazepoxide every 2-4 hours until they seem to be out of danger;

(b) Once delirium appears: 50-100 mg. Chlordiazepoxide should be given every four hours orally or I.M. (Intra-Muscular);

(c) High Caloric; high carbohydrate diet;

(d) Multi-vitamins;

(e) Should never be physically restrained If uncontrolled—a seclusion room can be used;

(f) Dehydration is corrected by IV (intravenous) fluids or oral fluids;

(g) Avoid phenothizines (tend to reduce seizure threshold);

(h) Warm, supportive psychotherapy; and

(i) Anti-convulsants are not useful in preventing of treating seizures. Use of chlordiazepoxide or diazepam is generally effective.

Alcohol Hallucinosis

Usually beginning within 48 hours after cessation of drinking and persisting after a person has recovered from symptoms of alcohol withdrawal.

Treatment

Benzodiazepines; Adequate Nutrition, Fluids, when this fails, antipsychotics may be used.

Korsakoff's Syndrome

Features: Short-term memory disturbance; Cerebraller signs; Peripheral Neuropathy; Cirrohosis of liver.

WERNICKE'S ENCEPHALOPATHY

Features: Ataxia, Nystagumus; Ophthalmoplegia; Confusion *Treatment of* Large doses of parental thiamine (Vitamin B1)

TREATMENT OF ALCOHOL DEPENDENCE

(I) Psychotheraphy, (ii) Medication: (a) Disulfiram (Antabuse) (b) Psychotropic Drugs.

ANTABUSE THERAPY

Antabuse competitively inhibits the enzyme aldehyde dehydrogenase, so that even a single drink of alcohol usually causes toxic reactions because of acetaldehyde accumulation in the blood.

Mechanism of Action:

Ethanol *Alcohol DH* ACEITALDEHYDE (Toxic) *Ald. D.H.* Ace tate- Antabuse inhibits

HO2 + COS

* Administration of Antabuse should not begin until 24 hrs. have elapsed since patient's last drink.
* Patient must be in good health.
* Highly motivated, co-operative; warn the patient about consequences of ingesting alcohol while on Antabuse or as long as two weeks thereafter.

After 250 mg, of Antabuse the effects are:
Flushing, feelings of heat in face, selera, upper limbs and chest; becomes pale, hypotension; Nausea; serious malaise, dizziness, blurred vision, palpitation; air hunger, numbness of extremities.

Contra-indications:

Absolute. First trimister of pregnancy Relative: I.H.D. Hepatic failure, peripheral Neuropathy; past H/O.Psychosis; Chronic renal failure.

***Serious Consequences:* (Toxicity of Disulfirm)**

Hepato toxicity; severe hypotension; marked tachycardia; toxic psychosis; memory impairment, confusion-disulfirm neuropathy; exacerbation of psychotic symptoms in Schizophrenia.
Controversial issues about disulfirmum-therapy:
(i) Dose, (ii) Duration of treatment, (iii) Utility of D.A.R.

PSYCHOTROPIC DRUGS

(i) Anti-anxiety Agents

(ii) Anti-depressants.

(iii) *Behaviour Therapy*: to teach alcoholic persons to reduce anxiety-relaxation training (P.M.R. or Savasana or T.M.) Assertive training; self-control skills; new strategies to master the environment;

Operant conditioning programmes to modify drinking behaviour or to stop. Reinforcers are—Monetary rewards; pleasurable social interaction; Avertive therapy.

(iv) Alcoholic anonymous (AA); Alanon-Organization for spouses of alcoholic persons; Alateen-Organization for children of alcoholics.

(v) *Half-way Homes*: The discharge of an alcoholic patient from the hospital often poses serious placement problems. Home or other familiar environment may be counter productive, unsupportive. The half-way house is an important treatment resource that provides emotional support, counselling and progressive entry into society.

CRAVING AND RELAPSE

One of the main factors to be dealt within the treatment of alcoholism is "Craving". Craving is an irresistible and uncontrollable urge to drink alcohol. If craving is adequately handled, the problem related to alcohol could be successfully managed. It is a difficult task as there is no specific or definite ways and means of achieving the victory over craving. Counselling helps to overcome craving. During critical periods of craving the alcoholics are advised to take substantial amounts of food.

Other suggestions are:

— Diversion of mind in other activities like going for a walk with other family members, watching TV/Video, listening to music, gardening, cooking, reading books etc.

— Engaging in recreational activity.

— Yoga or meditation

— Participate in religious activities

— Avoid negatively stimulating environments, lonely walks, company of other alcoholics, idle moments, keeping more money with them.

— Intense craving is seen on pay days, social get-together celebrations, picnics, holiday outings, and arrival of friends/relatives.

Relapse:

Return to a pathological pattern of alcohol abuse after a period of voluntary abstinence.

Relapse rate is 33 to 64 per cent.

Relapse is not unpredictable and not to a treatment failure. Treatment of alcohol dependence should not be only abstinence. It should include social, occupational, recreational rehabilitation.

Phases in Relapse:

(i) Procontemplation; (ii) Contemplation; (iii) Determination; (iv) Action Phase; (v) State of maintenance (Drug free state); (vi) Relapse.

Reasons for Relapse:

Availability, socio-cultural norms, biological and psychological reasons.

Prevention:

(i) Self-control; (ii) Minimal Intervention; (iii) Manipulation of substance/person/environment; (iv) Full scale intervention.

10

ARRACK DRINKING AS A HEALTH HAZARD—PRIMARY HEALTH CARE APPROACH AS SOLUTION

T.A.V. Narayana Raju

Problems related to abuse of alcohol are rapidly increasing almost everywhere. It has become one of the most widespread, deadly and serious public health problems of this century. It is influencing more people and broader age groups than even before. The Director General of WHO noted recently when he commented that of all the so called drugs of abuse, alcohol is the most frequently abused and alcohol remains the cause of the greatest number of health and social problems. The abuse of alcohol constitutes one of the main causes of impairment of social competence and performance. In healthy young people, behavioural problems associated with alcohol are currently the most important reasons for interrupted social and intellectual development. On the road and at home or place of work it has become a leading cause of accidents or injuries. It is becoming a very dangerous and crucial factor in breakdown of families.

India is on the verge of an epidemic. 7.5 million people are said to have some form of ill-health due to consumption of alcohol.

Alcohol acts as a sedative or depressant when it is stopped, sometime after a period of use, a withdrawal syndrome with unpleasant symptoms may develop. Alcohol is thought to have stimulant properties, like aggressive behaviour, which actually occurs because it depresses the inhibitory centres of the brain before the excitatory centres. Alcohol acts on fat filled membranes in nervous tissues in brain. Metabolic tolerance may develop following a period of regular consumption. Many studies backed by clinical experience, suggest that people with severe complications resulting from alcohol have psychological or psychiatric problems, as a cause or a result. However, powerful the biological and psychological determinants of addiction, may be, social factors are also of critical importance. Attitudes to the consumption or related problems may range from intolerance to permissiveness, which may also change with time.

Prevention of the Problem

Consumption of alcohol can be reduced at the societal level by restricting supply and decreasing the demand. Supply can be regulated by controlling the number and type of outlets and effectively banning consumption of alcohol by persons below a certain age.

There is need for an attitudinal change in the society in general to decrease demand for alcohol. Mass campaigns, education programmes in schools, special attention to high risk groups are some of the ways to achieve the objective. Education of the young to resist peer pressure and regulation of advertisements are also effective. Public opinion can be swayed through advertising campaigns by Government warning of the consequences of the use of alcohol.

Caring for the Individuals

Help is often provided by relatives, friends, neighbours and community agencies with their health and welfare professionals, of which treatment also is a part. There should be efforts at promotion of a capacity to cope with wavering motivation in problem cases. Services of treatment should be extended to all those people who consume alcohol but do not show any complications, by way of minor intervention at an early stage.

Detoxification is the first thing done in treatment for intoxication or help withdrawing from alcohol. Simple measures like encouragement and reassurance will also help in the process. Today the treatment of the outpatient is also found equally effective. Since alcohol related problems have psychological, biological and social components, a holistic and comprehensive approach is needed to tackle the problems covering not only alcohol users but also people at risk and the community. There is a need to review the problem in a P.H.C. setting.

Why Primary Care setting?

— It is too widespread a problem to be dealt with by a small specialised service, which is difficult.

— Alcoholics visit more often primary care centres.

— Early detection and treatment are more likely.

— Primary health care facilitates contact with the family and the community.

The current trend of decentralizing health care services as much as possible to the community provides opportunities for workers to play a leading role in the management of the problems of the abuse of alcohol.

As a first step assessment of problem is done through interview of the individual and his family,

— to obtain accurate information about alcohol use and physical illnesses, social or psychological problems.

— to identify strengths and weaknesses of individual and his family and their ability to cope with problems.

Alcohol problems in the family, especially among parents, may go unnoticed for years, while individual members continue to experience stress.

Proper assessment provides basis for right action. The commonly used strategy for treatment is

— improving social relationships and supports,

— developing confidence in ability to change,

— identifying reasons to change,

— developing alternative activities,

— learning to prevent relapse.

The various methods used for assessment are

— to collect existing information at health centre/ hospital,

— to interview knowledgeable key informants,

— to make participant observation,

— to organise a general population survey.

Organizing Primary Health Care Services to Combat Alcohol Abuse

— Medical science and technology are appropriate for treating individual diseases but not sufficient to reduce and prevent alcohol related problems.

— Decentralized care is necessary for the promotion of health, prevention of disease, active participation of family and community, involving non-specialised primary care workers and collaboration with other Governmental and non-governmental organisations. Great emphasis should be laid on the need for transfer of knowledge and skills to primary health care workers and to people themselves. They should be trained in simple but effective techniques to manage alcohol related problems, mobilizing community action, encouraging healthy life styles, stimulating self-help groups, providing health education, interviewing and counselling, providing guidance about use of leisure time.

New Role for the Specialist:

— Educate, facilitate, stimulate

— Consult on difficult cases

— Support and motivate PHC workers

— Transfer skills

— Coordinate and evaluate

— Plan and monitor policies

— Become advocate and adviser

Lastly, there is a greater need to mobilise the community to reduce the abuse of alcohol. Changes in behaviour can only be brought about and sustained if the community becomes actively involved in promoting good health. A community action team (CAT) should be formed with representatives of health sector, business, social services, voluntary bodies, parents and teachers. The team should pursue the various measures suggested with enthusiasm to create awareness by organizing youth programmes, accident prevention campaigns and the like.

Table 2

Distribution of Households by Income Group and Percentage Group of Expenditure on Alcohol to Total Household Income

S.No.	Income Group (Rs.)	Percentage Group of Alcohol Expenditure to Total HH Income							
		0	0-10	11-20	21-30	31-40	41-50	51 & Above	Total
1.	0 - 400	28	3	1	—	—	—	2	34
		(82.35)	(8.82)	(2.95)				(5.88)	(100.00)
2.	401 - 800	107	46	25	12	6	5	6	207
		(51.69)	(22.22)	(12.08)	(5.79)	(2.90)	(2.42)	(2.90)	(100.00)
3.	801 - 1200	66	44	19	6	3	2	2	142
		(46.49)	(30.98)	(13.38)	(4.22)	(2.11)	(1.41)	(1.41)	(100.00)
4.	1201 - 1600	65	27	18	1	1	1	—	113
		(57.52)	(23.89)	(15.93)	(0.88)	(0.88)	(0.88)		(100.00)
5.	1601 and above	61	30	19	3	1	—	2	116
		(52.59)	(25.86)	(16.38)	(2.59)	(0.86)		(1.72)	(100.00)
	Total	327	150	82	22	11	8	12	612
		(53.43)	(24.51)	(13.41)	(3.59)	(1.79)	(1.31)	(1.96)	(100.00)

Table 3
Perhousehold Monthly Expenditure on Alcohol by Income Group

Sl. No.	*Income Group (Rs.)*	*Sample HHs*		*Population*		*No. of Alcohol consumeing HHs*	*% of Alcohol consuming HHs*	*Per HH. Income (Rs.)*	*Per HH Alcohol Expenditure*	*% of Alcohol Expenditure to Total HH. Income*
		No.	*%*	*No.*	*%*					
1.	Below 400	34	5.56	113	3.91	6	17.65	287	171	59.58
2.	401-800	207	33.82	868	10.04	100	48.31	588	121	20.58
3.	801-1200	142	23.20	676	23.40	76	53.52	983	175	17.80
4.	1201-1600	113	18.46	557	19.28	48	42.48	1360	184	13.52
5.	1601 & above	116	18.95	675	23.36	55	47.41	2184	298	13.64
	Total	612	100.00	2889	100.00	285	46.57	1108	181	16.34

Table 4
Distribution of Households by Caste Groups and Percentage Group of Alcohol Expenditure to Total Household Income

S. No.	Caste Group	*Percentage Group of Alcohol Expenditure to Total Household Income* 0	1-10	11-20	21-30	31-40	41-50	51 & Above	Total No. of HHs.
1.	F.C.	31 (64.58)	9 (18.75)	6 (12.50)	-	-	-	2 (4.17)	48 (100.00)
2.	B.C.	227 (53.92)	99 (23.52)	56 (13.30)	17 (4.40)	10 (2.38)	5 (1.19)	7 (1.66)	421 (100.00)
3.	S.C.	62 (47.33)	39 (29.77)	18 (13.74)	5 (3.82)	1 (0.76)	3 (2.29)	3 (2.29)	131 (100.00)
4.	S.T.	1 (33.33)	2 (66.67)	-	-	-	-	-	3 (100.00)
5.	Others	6 (66.67)	1 (11.11)	2 (22.22)	-	-	-	-	9 (100.00)
	Total	327 (53.43)	150 (24.51)	82 (13.41)	22 (3.59)	11 (1.79)	8 (1.31)	12 (1.96)	612 (100.00)

Table 5
Per Household Monthly Consumption of Alcohol by Caste Groups

Sl. No.	*Caste*	*Sample HHs*		*Population*		*No. of Alcohol consuming HHs*	*% of Alcohol consuming HHs*	*Per HH. Income (Rs.)*	*Per HH Alcohol Expenditure (Rs.)*	*% of Alcohol Expenditure to Total HH. Income*
		No.	*%*	*No.*	*%*					
1.	F.C.	48	7.84	201	6.96	17	35.42	1055	229	21.71
2.	B.C.	421	68.79	2021	69.96	194	46.08	1156	201	17.39
3.	S.C.	131	21.41	608	21.05	69	52.67	942	132	14.01
4.	S.T.	3	0.49	11	0.38	2	66.67	970	120	12.37
5.	Others	9	1.47	48	1.66	3	33.33	1548	120	7.75
		612	100.00	2889	100.00	285	46.57	1108	181	16.34

11

ALCOHOL POLICIES AND URBAN POOR

G. Ramachandrudu
Ch. Appa Rao
A.L.V. Kartikeye

Prohibition has once again come to the central stage of national agenda, not because the welfare state wanted it, nor academics highlighted the evils of cancerous growth of alcoholism, but because the rural neo-literate and illiterate women belonging to the weaker sections of the Nellore district of Andhra Pradesh raised their voice against the liquor barons who are promoting liquor trade indiscriminately and slowly infiltrating into the top political brass of the country. This historic women's movement unfortunately had been politicised and diluted.

For decades prohibitionists had based their agitation against the liquor traffic upon purely moral and sociological grounds. They had declared that alcohol destroyed the soul, broke up homes, and bred brutality and crime. The third dimension of alcoholism is health and productivity. The WHO pointed out that if we are serious about the goal of health for all by the year 2000 AD, then we cannot afford to ignore alcohol related problems. The production and consumption of alcohol leads to wastage of scarce resources and decreases productivity of labour and also to the commitment of health service resources to the treatment of people with alcohol related diseases and other problems like accidents, fires and criminal acts.

Generally it is believed that the prevalence of alcoholism is predominant among lower income groups and lower-social strata of the society. The empirical evidence regarding alcohol consumption by different social or economic groups for recent years is scarce. We have made an attempt to fill this gap. This paper attempts to analyse the alcohol expenditure data of slum dwellers by social and income groups. It also discusses the alcohol policies to be followed by the Government in order to avoid economic, social and political chaos in the long run, if the present trends of alcohol consumption continue.

Data Base and Limitations

Data on the household consumption particulars are drawn from the Evaluation Study of the Visakhapatnam Slum Improvement Project (VSIP), sponsored by the ODA (UK) and VMC and conducted by the IDPS, Visakhapatnam, during 1991-92. The socio-economic survey of households as a part of the Evaluation Study has adopted the panel survey methodology. Under this method, the same households visited once in the base period (1988) is visited again in 1991 after three years of the implementation of the VSIP. The panel study enables the researcher to measure not only the net changes during the period but also to identify and study the changers.

Monthly alcohol consumption expenditure was noted for the entire household, but not by person. Thus we could identify households but not persons consuming alcohol, both in 1988 and 1991.

Changes in the Alcohol Consumption Patterns

Panel survey methodology is useful to prepare a turnover table in order to identify not only gross as well as net changes, but also to study the changers in alcohol consumption during 1988-91. Table 1 presents data in the Turnover Table which clearly brings out the shift in the alcohol consumption. Figures in brackets are the percentages in the total sample (n=612).

Table 1
Turnover Table for HHs Reporting Alcohol consumption

	1988		
	Consuming	Not Consuming	Total
1991			
Consuming	36	249	285
	(5.88)	(40.69)	(46.57)
Not Consuming	53	274	327
	(8.66)	(44.77)	(53.43)
Total	89	523	612
	(14.54)	(85.46)	(100.00)

Thus, during the three year period there was an alarming increase (40.69 per cent) of alcohol consuming households, who entered afresh into alcoholism. This percentage will be more if we consider the individuals consuming alcohol, instead of households.

Fifty three out of eighty nine reporting discontinuation of alcohol consumption are non-migrants, Forward Castes and higher income groups. On the other hand, a majority of the households reporting alcohol consumption afresh in 1991 (249) are migrants, BCs and SCs, and lower income groups.

Alcohol Consumption by Monthly Household Income Groups:

Table 2 presents the distribution of households by income group and percentage of alcohol expenditure to total household income. Out of 612 sample households, 327 (53.43 per cent) households did not report any expenditure on alcohol and hence they are considered as non-alcohol consuming households. It is interesting to note from the table, that out of 34 hhs. in the lowest income group of Rs. 400 and below, 28 (82.35 per cent) have not reported to have any expenditure on alcohol. In the highest income group of Rs. 1601 and above, out of 116 hhs, 61 (52.59 per cent) households have not reported any expenditure on alcohol. The lowest percentage of non-alcohol consuming households (46 per cent) is reported in the income group of Rs. 801-1200.

Table 2 also presents the distribution of households by percentage of alcohol expenditure to total household income. In all the income groups, for majority of the households the percentage of alcohol expenditure was less than 10 per cent of the monthly household income. The least percentage of households is the lowest income group of less than Rs. 400. But, even though there are less number of alcohol consuming households, their percentage expenditure on alcohol is higher than those of other income groups. If we look at the highest percentage group of 51 and above, we find the highest percentage of households (5.88 per cent) belong to the lowest income group. This clearly shows the severe impact of alcohol consumption on the budgets of lowest income groups.

Table 3 presents per household monthly expenditure on alcohol by income groups and their percentage to the total expenditure. While the average expenditure for all the households is Rs. 181, the lowest income group spends Rs. 171 and the highest income group spends Rs. 298 per month. The percentage share of this expenditure on monthly income is the highest among the households in the lowest income group and is as high as 59.58, while the average is 16.34.

Alcohol Consumption by Caste Groups

Table 4 presents the distribution of households by caste

group and percentage of alcohol expenditure to total household income. As there are vast differences in the number of households in each caste group, caste differentials must be interpreted with a great care. Thus among the three major caste groups of FC, BC, and SCs, it is among FCs alcohol drinking is less prevalent and it is more among SCs. This evidence supports the widely believed opinion that the lower social groups have higher prevalence rate of alcohol consumption.

Table 4 also presents the distribution of households by percentage of alcohol expenditure to total household income. In all the caste groups, vast majority of the households spend less than 10 per cent of their monthly household income. Almost same proportion of households are found in the second percentage group of 11-20 among the three major caste groups of FC, BC and SCs. Quite interestingly 4 per cent of the FC category spend more than 51 per cent of their income, which is the highest among all the caste groups. Among SCs 2.29 per cent of households spend the similar amount on alcohol.

Table 5 presents per household monthly expenditure on alcohol by income groups and their percentage to the total expenditure. The percentage share of this expenditure on monthly income is the highest among FCs (21.71 per cent). The BCs, SCs and STs spend 17.39 per cent, 14.01 per cent and 12.37 per cent respectively, while the aggregate percentage of alcohol expenditure to the total income is 16.34 per cent.

Alcohol Policies

Alcohol is the oldest and widely used intoxicating substance known to man. Not only historical documentary evidence but also archaeological artefacts reveal that the use of alcoholic beverages has roots that go back to the earliest stages of man's development. For the periods for which pictorial and written records are available, it is clear that the production and consumption of alcohol was integrated into social and religious life in many communities in different parts of the world. In India, even today, alcohol consumption is a way of life in certain ethnic groups in the urban, rural and tribal areas. British rule brought the culture of alcohol to the elite sections of the Indian society and this has an enormous demonstration effect on middle and lower income classes of the society. Rapid growth of alcohol consumption results in crime and violence, which is a matter of serious concern to the modern welfare state, the state tended to impose controls of varied nature alcohol consumption.

Alcohol policies have to be sensitive to the history of the country, its culture and its drinking practices. They require imagination, tolerance and a sense of vision. Of course, the two extreme policy measures are: (a) total prohibition and (b) laissez-faire. While total prohibition is an utopian concept, laissez-faire in alcohol is suicidal. Therefore, there is a need for designing an appropriate alcohol policy, which should be regional, social and health specific. The twin arguments against prohibition, viz., the loss of revenue and the failure of the Government to prevent the production and distribution of illicit liquor, are not socially and politically justifiable keeping in view the heavy social, economic and health costs of alcoholism. Therefore, to start with, the Government should announce the following regulations on alcohol sale practices:

(a) the location and opening hours of retail outlets,

(b) legal drinking age,

(c) restaurant practices,

(d) restrictions of the right to sell alcohol and

(e) alcohol price policy aimed at achieving minimum consumption.

Increasing number of social science research works provide evidence that the awareness among women due to the spread of literacy would help to solve the long pending social problems like prostitution, dowry, child labour and age at marriage against which there are already enough legislative controls. In this light, the current women's movement against alcoholism is not only an indication but also a ray of hope for a better social, economic and political order in India.

12

DE-ADDICTION AMONG ALCOHOLICS—A CASE STUDY IN VISAKHAPATNAM

—B. Ratna Kumari

Drug abuse has taken alarming proportions and presently it is the biggest global problem of civilised societies. It spreads darkness to the families and make them deteriorated day by day in all aspects of their life. There are many efforts done by voluntary organisations and various institutions to drive away this bad element from the society. But the results are not significant and this is the time to take strong policy matters against Alcoholism.

The present study is confined to the impact of Alcoholism on the industrial worker, his family and his work environment. It also analyses the impact of 'De-Addiction Programme' and its programme package, with reference to the de-addiction programme in Bharat Heavy Plate and Vessels Ltd. (BHPV), Visakhapatnam, a public undertaking, from 1985 onwards. The researcher enquired the industrial workers and supervisors through personal interviews and concluded with suggestion for the successful implementation of De-Addiction Programmes in Bharat Heavy Plate and Vessels Ltd. (BHPV).

Definition of Alcoholism

Alcoholism is the third largest killer disease in the world, the first and second being heart disease and cancer. Alcoholism is a major organisational problem leading to absenteeism, indiscipline and less productivity. It generates noticeable mental disturbances in alcoholics and interferes with his physical and mental health. The alcoholic's inter-personal relations, social and economic functions are also affected.

Alcoholism affects an industrial worker in many ways and leaves him bankrupt. Alcoholism is a chronic illness psychic, somatic or psychosomatic, which manifests itself as a disorder of behaviour.[1] The best available data indicates that alcoholics constitute atleast 5 per cent of the total workforce in industry in many countries.[2]

Labour welfare is one of the major aspect of national programmes towards bettering the lot of labour and creating a life and work environment of decent comfort for this class of population.[3] These are meant not only to provide material benefits but also to promote the real welfare of the labour. BHPV was established in the year 1966 to manufacture process plant equipment for fertilisers, chemical, petroleum and allied industries, etc. After twentysix years of its functioning BHPV has today emerged as one of the country's largest fabricator of equipment for process plants. The noble philosophy of labour welfare was ingrained in the BHPV authorities with a view 'to help the worker when he is down without much concern for what brought him down?' The BHPV introduced the De-Addiction Programme since 1985 due to the following reasons: Alcoholics absent from work on the average three-and-a-half times more than other workers. They receive upto three times more in sick payments and affect the efficiency of fellow employees in their shifts. They had 2-4 times more accidents at work. About 98 per cent of the addicts had the history of

1. Medical Times, March, 1991, p.3.
2. Ibid.
3. Bhagoliwal, T.N. "Economics of Labour and Industrial Relations," 1983.

unauthorised absence and 15-45 per cent disciplinary cases have relationship with alcohol users. About 80 per cent of addicts used to fight with personnel in the Finance Department with regard to advances of various kinds.

As the alcoholics need fair treatment and are to be given the opportunity to seek help. T. Gokulum, Dy.Manager (HRD) thought of a scheme to liberate the chronic alcoholics from the clutches of money lenders and also from the dreadful habit of chronic alcoholism. The de-addiction scheme is in vogue from May, 1985 and gained momentum with assistance of Dr.G. Bhagya Rao, Psychiatrist and Dr. S.Subba Rao, and all Departmental Officers supported the scheme with their staff. Before discussing the de-addiction programme, it is meaningful to know what is meant by 'Addiction.'

What is Addiction?

Addiction is characterised by: (i) an overpowering desire or need (compulsion) to continue taking drugs and to obtain them by any means, (ii) tendency to increase dose, and (iii) psychic and sometimes physical dependence on drugs.

Drug addiction is basically a psycho-social problem which not only creates physical and psychic dependence but also changes personality patterns, hampers social functioning and adjustment, and leads to psycho-physiological discomforts. The correlation between psychological and psysiological dependency creates a vicious circle in which an addict rolls like a rolling stone and for him it is difficult to break this circle.

An addict's emotional drives and needs compel him to consume drugs either to experience psychic effects or to avoid discomforts due to its absence, or both, which ultimately create physical dependence in terms of increasing quantity, repetition with higher periodicity and vice versa. Though drug abusers take drugs at the first time for enjoying psychic effects or to suppress unconscious emotions, fears, anxiety etc., they are likely to have a weak ego structure, defective super ego functioning, inadequate identification, lack of realistic orientation towards the future and mistrust towards social-institutions. The problems caused by alcoholism in all the three areas—health, social and economic—are of serious nature and they directly or indirectly drive him to poverty which is his own making, because an industrial worker is well paid with several fringe benefits. This poverty again leads him to drinking and it is a continuous vicious circle that has to be broken at some point by some external force. Hence, treatment models of drug addicts must be more and more psycho-socially oriented.

The Problems of Alcoholics:

A. Health:

Some of the chronic health problems associated with alcoholism are gastritis, cardionyopaltry, neuritis fatty liver, cirrhosis, tuberculosis and psychosis apart from tremors of limbs, sleep disorders, blackouts, nausea, hallucinations, impaired judgement, paranoia and the potential vulnerability to accidents.

In the survey of BHPV de-addiction programme, it has been observed that the alcoholics had great impact on health. 80 per cent of the total subjects had developed physical complications and before being enrolled in the programme, they were suffering from various problems including TB, jaundice, vitamin deficiencies, lever disorders, psychotic symptoms like hallucinations, paranoia, anxiety, convulsions, delirium, tremors and sleep disorders.

B. Work

Alcohol affects social life of the individual with poorly developed social skills leading to bad working relationships, bad time keepings, long lunch breaks, poor concentration, change of jobs, lost time, lower productivity, absenteeism, inefficiency, frequent accidents, disputes, grievances and loss of job.

In the sample survey, it is found that 90 per cent of the addicts were absenting from duty and it was frequent after the weekends or pay days. It was observed they have frequent sick absences and unexplained absences. 90 per cent had bad time keeping. This absenteeism is 2 to 3 times more compared to other absentees. There was deterioration in standards, quality and quantity of work, work efficiency and judgement of alcoholic worker. There was loss of interest in work and failure to meet deadlines. The uninhibited behaviour along with inefficiency gave rise to misunderstanding with supervisors in 65 per cent of cases. More than 75 per cent of the addicts received memos for their misbehaviour. Even the colleagues were often identified as hostile by 70 per cent of the addicts. Increased irritability, nervousness and argumentativeness on the part of the alcoholic were reported by supervisors and co-workers. The supervisors reported that 65 per cent of addicts showed unsatisfactory, hostile or quarrel-some behaviour with co-workers. Between 20 and 25 per cent of accidents at work places involve intoxicated persons resulting in injuries to themselves and to others. They have 2 to 4 times more accidents than other employees. So they claim sickness and other disablement benefits 2-3 times more. About 98 per cent of the addicts had a history of unauthorised absence and 15-45 per cent disciplinary cases have relationship with alcohol use. About 80 per cent of addicts would fight with personnel in the Finance Dept. with regard to advances of various kinds.

C. Family

Alcoholism leaves tremendous emotional impact on the family. Excessive drinking causes frequent quarrels at home, strained relationships, child neglect and broken marriages.

In the survey, it has been observed that 80 per cent claimed that they had conflicts with wife, brothers and parents. 94 per cent used to beat wives when drunk and would abuse and assault children and had asked them to leave the house. The family was involved in many ways like drunken behaviour at home, financial burden on the family, lack of care about family needs, strained interpersonal relations with wife and in a few cases (3 per cent) contributed to destabilization of family life. Almost all had quarrelled with wife over the expenditure on drinks. 40 per cent of the wives of these addicts were upset about husband's drinking and resultant financial crisis and were worried about children. 22 per cent of the addicts had extra-marital relations, 70 per cent of alcoholics ended up making promises which they never kept.

About 85 per cent of the addicts never showed any concern about their children neither bothered for their studies nor looked after their needs, because of their drunken behaviour at home. Children of 50 per cent addicts discontinued their studies because they were not provided with text books on time. 70 per cent of children of the addicts had negative feeling towards their fathers due to alcoholism.

D. Economic Status

Low levels of income and savings, innumerable recoveries from the company, debts interest paying, credits in all stores, pawning of jewellery and other valuable articles, selling away movable and immovable property, depending on wife's earnings and low standard of living.

In the survey, it has been observed that about 98 per cent of alcoholics were getting Rs. 150 to Rs. 300 as their take home pay after all deductions. The reasons behind this were, they incurred huge amounts of debts from official and co-operative institutions. Also 70 per cent of them had borrowed money with high interest from private money lenders and 60 per cent of addicts derived money for mortgaging and selling the property and from wife's earnings. In the beginning, the standard of living was low in 95 per cent as they would spend Rs. 250 to Rs, 300 for total family members.

All the physical, psychological, social and economic problems are interdependent and are mainly due to alcoholism. Since there are problems in drinking process, programme for alcohol de-addiction for industrial workers is an innovative approach and it is a part of human resources development (HRD). This programme is to be based on the belief that alcoholism is a treatable disease.

De-Addiction Programme as the Road to Recovery

Addiction cannot be cured merely by prescribing drugs. Sometimes hospitalisation becomes necessary for restricting physical dependence on drugs but drugs alone cannot be a solution as most of the drugs produce dependency. Hence there is a need for supportive therapies. The de-addiction programme entails three levels of prevention, i.e., primary, secondary and tertiary.

The Programme aims at

(i) Informing and educating all levels of staff about the dangers and problems associated with alcohol use (counselling), particularly the risks while at work;

(ii) to inform the staff of the services and programmes available;

(iii) to emphasise the need of the programme in the interest of the welfare of the employee and his family; and

(iv) providing treatment for the alcoholics and facilitate social and psychological rehabilitation.

Components of the Programme

(i) Crisis intervention in the medical, psychological or social emergency;

(ii) Control of dysfunctional behaviour;

(iii) Individual, group and family therapy;

(iv) Rehabilitation to settle in the work, to regain working habits, to accustom to demands of a full day's work, to train in new skills;

(v) Follow-up action: person to person meetings;

(vi) A therapy against the fear of relapse;

(vii) Feedback by corresponding with ex-addicts;

(viii) Field survey of ex-addicts; and,

(ix) Community support and involvement.

Impact of the De-addiction Programme on Workers

In the present study, an attempt has been made to study the impact of de-addiction programme in four areas, viz., health, financial status, family and work environment of the addicts by comparing their status in these four areas before and after being enrolled in deaddiction programme.

The details of the number of workers enrolled in the programme, and the amount which was met by BHPV Management and the number of beneficiaries of this programme are given in the following Table 1:

Table 1
An Assessment of the Effect of the Programme on the Worker during the period 1985-1991

Year	Amount spent on this programme	No. of Alcoholics	No. of Beneficiaries
1985	25,000	76	65
1986	25,000	34	30
1987	25,000	17	12
1988	25,000	16	10
1989	25,000	10	8
1990	25,000	8	5
1991	25,000	7	5
	1,75,000	168	135

Source: Reports from Mrs. N. Indira Rani, Medico-Social Programme Officer of BHPV.

Profile of the Addicts in BHPV

It is evident from the above table and the demographic profiles of the workers that all of them belong to labour category and are doing technical jobs and 95 per cent of them are from highly skilled to semi-skilled involved in welding, fitting, gas cutting, crane operators, etc. 90 per cent of them had good reputation for their work at the workspot. The grade of salary is from Rs. 900 to Rs. 2000 and they belong to nuclear family. Among the total workers involved in the addiction programme, 80 per cent belong to the age group of 35-45 years, 53.4 per cent have the habit of day-time drinking and 76 per cent used to drink while on work. 74 per cent mentioned that they had started taking alcohol as social drinking and only 26 per cent had personal reasons like death of close family members, mostly spouse or child, involvement in arrack preparation and employment in occupations which permit drinking, namely, military police, welding jobs and agricultural work. All the workers are married and 80 per cent had financial problems and incurred debts from Rs. 5,000 to Rs. 25,000. Fifty per cent of them had serious family conflicts and 2 per cent had separations.

It is noted from the Table 1, that the total number of alcoholics declined from 76 in 1985 to 7 in 1991 and the total number of beneficiaries also increased, even though the number of alcoholic workers declined substantially. It is known that the cost of medicines met from hospital budget on an average was of Rs. 5,000 for anti-alcohol table for one year. Other supporting drugs are also given at an average of Rs. 5,000 per year.

The de-addiction programme started with a team consisting of Psychiatrist, Medical Officer, Social Worker and Administrative Officer and they conducted the programme in the hospital. The cases were enrolled and all the necessary investigations were carried out and the physical problems were paid utmost attention. Apart from anti-addict drug the addicts were given hospitalisation for the first 10 days, glucose, vitamins and other nutrients to improve the general health and were prescribed medicines for specific symptoms. Within two months of starting treatment the health of the 90 per cent of addicts has come to normalcy, and a few cases needed long term treatment in cases like T.B.

An assessment of the effect of the programme on the worker during the last seven years shows that:

50 per cent reduction in occupational injuries, 60 per cent reduction in sickness and accident benefit payments and 50 per cent reduction in grievances and disciplinary action. This percentage is related to the total percentage of workers.

Among addicts it was assessed that: 80 per cent reduction in absenteeism, 40 per cent reduction in time lost, 60 per cent of increased earnings, 90 per cent of restoring to normal health, 70 per cent improved family and co-worker relationship, 75 per cent improved productivity, 80 per cent savings resulting in the acquisition of jewellery, sites and houses, and 60 per cent of the de-addicts are receiving incentives and average take home pay become Rs. 1000 to Rs. 1500 and more.

Regarding the performance of de-addiction programmes at BHPV, 200 alcoholics were identified and 168 joined the scheme so far either by themselves or pressurised by either family or managers. Out of 168 there are 33 drop-outs who have deteriorated severely. There are a few workers who occasionally relapse and are yet to be stabilised. On the whole the rate of success is 75 per cent and, the efforts made by the management are highly appreciable.

Conclusion

Those persons who are addicted to excessive consumption of alcohol suffers from ill-health, inefficiency, poverty, etc. So, his family suffers, the productivity suffers, the organisation suffers and projected to the national level the country's economy suffers. While the State tries to prevent the occurrence of poverty among people of different sectors and much money is spent on welfare schemes, these become futile, unless and until the social evils like alcoholism are eradicated totally from the society. The eradication programmes including de-addiction must be taken up at organisational, State and Central levels.

In a State where the class movement and the dalit movement have been paving newer ways, the anti-liquor movement, started and led by women has shocked many patriarchs irrespective of their caste, class and status.

However, it is still a movement that attempts to assert the mother's right to set the family right and the attempts of patriarchal society is to see that it shall not become a feminist movement where it formulates its own theoretical framework and practical programme just as the class and anti-caste movements in the State have done. The repeated attempts to define this movement as part of class movement, or to define it as part of anti-caste movement, because majority of women participating in the movement are SCs and BCs, indicate that many have not yet come to accept that it is in fact a 'prelude' to a 'matriarchal revolution' which may in the long run pose major questions for feminism.

Whether one likes it or not the women cadres and leaders emerging from this movement will pose serious questions in future. The questions that the women of grass roots level pose to husbands, activists and parties—to the entire civil society—will be radically different from the ones that the urban middle class women have posed so far.

BIBLIOGRAPHY

Bhagoliwal T.N.: *Economics of Labour and Industrial Relations*, 1983.
Medical Times, March, 1991.
Ibid
Snajai Bhatt & Madhu Bhatt: "*De-Addiction: The Road to Recovery*," Social Welfare, Vol. 38, No. 6, Sept. 1991, pp. 11-13.

13

ARRACK DRINKERS AND THEIR ATTITUDES TOWARDS PROHIBITION

Dr. B. Madhukar Patnaik

The agitation by women against arrack auctions and sales in Andhra Pradesh is gaining its momentum and has already become a major issue of political discussion in the State. The movement led by fearless and courageous rural women-folk is also being supported by eminent people from all walks of life. The context is whether to ban the arrack auctions and sales or to continue. This has become a critical debating issue between the Government and the agitators. While the Government has become concerned about the ways and means to fill the deficit of Rs. 800 crores and above in its revenue if prohibition is imposed; the agitating women on the other hand are worried about the future of their children and families. In this connection it is also necessary to know more about the drinking practices and reasons for drinking and the attitudes of drinkers who are mostly men towards prohibition. There is need for a careful study of this aspect in discussing the subject of anti-arrack agitation and demand for prohibition.

Hence, an attempt is made to study the drinking practices and reasons for drinking and attitudes towards prohibition of drinkers, specifically arrack drinkers, in Visakhapatnam city. The specific objectives of the study undertaken are as follows:

1. To analyse the socio-economic characteristics of drinking respondents;
2. To examine their drinking practices;
3. To discuss their attitudes towards prohibition of arrack sales; and
4. To draw a few policy conclusions regarding eradication of drinking habit among the drinkers.

Design of the Study

Keeping in view the above objectives, an attempt is made to conduct an on-the-spot survey by canvassing a structured schedule to a large number of drinkers near an arrack shop in the city. For this purpose, the arrack shop of Isukathota area has been purposely selected as it is situated in a busy traffic junction and customers belonging to many occupational categories visit the shop.

Primarily, it is aimed to collect data from 100 respondents but we could succeed in collecting information from 20 drinkers only. The main reasons are: (i) Hostility of the shop-keeper to canvasing of schedule within his premises; (ii) Impossibility of individual interviews as the group crowds around the interviewer; and (iii) the unwillingness of the respondent to be interviewed in the midst of a group. Similar problems were faced when we tried to interview arrack consumers in another shop. Therefore, we shifted partly from individual interviews to group interviews, especially on attitudes to prohibition, drinking practices, and awareness of detriment to health.

Results of the interviews are presented under the following sections:

I. Socio-economic characteristics of drinkers;

II. Arrack drinking practices and reasons for drinking; and,

III. Attitudes of arrack drinkers towards prohibition.

The concluding part suggests some suitable measures based on the above analysis for eradication of drinking habit among the drinkers.

Socio-Economic Characteristics of Drinkers

The centre in which the shop is located is very busy right from 5.30 AM to 9.30 PM. Another significant feature is that it is a centre at which labourers seeking daily wages gather and are picked up by employers.

The selected arrack shop is situated in a small hut with elevated roof. An old woman sells *kababs* and other food items for the drinkers. The shop is kept open continuously from 5.30 AM to 11.00 PM. It is very busy in the evening from 6.00 PM to 9 PM, when labourers return from their work after receiving the daily wages.

For describing the characteristics of the drinkers and drinking practices, we chose two methods; participatory observation and secondly interviews.

Majority of the customers are daily wage labourers. The customers stay for a very short period in the shop. They rush into the shop with sufficient money in their hands and exit immediately after having a peg or two. Rickshaw-pullers and other cart-pullers park their vehicles on the road itself, consume the drinks quickly and go back to their own work. Most of the drinkers drink without diluting the liquor and without any munching material. Most of the daily wage labourers belong to the nearby places.

In the group interviews, the discussion related to demographic particulars, occupational status and income levels of the respondents. They were also questioned on the usual time of reaching home after a day's hard work. The observations are as follows:

(i) A majority of the respondents are reported to be in the age group of 25-45 years from the illiterate backward class communities.

(ii) Almost all the respondents are married and residing with their family members with an average family size of more than four. Further, they are also reported to be as heads of their respective families.

(iii) With regard to their occupational status, more than 50 per cent of the participants are reported to be daily wage labourers such as construction workers, rickshaw pullers, luggage carriers, etc., in the informal sector followed by monthly salaried Class-IV employees from the organised sector and a few self-employed having petty establishments.

(iv) The income levels of the respondents are reported to be ranging between Rs. 25 and Rs. 50 for daily wage labourers, between Rs. 1400 and Rs. 2500 for monthly salaried Class-IV employees and, from Rs. 35 to Rs. 100 per day for the self-employed.

(v) Regarding the usual time of reaching their homes after visiting the shop it is before 7.30 PM for daily wage labourers, between 8.30 PM and 9.30 PM for monthly salaried employees and no such definite time is reported by the self-employed petty traders.

(vi) A further enquiry on the above timings revealed that a majority of the daily wage labourers are from the outskirts of the city. They usually leave their work places around 5.30 PM in the evening and catch the city bus to reach nearby markets. After purchasing the daily required commodities, they pay a visit to the nearby arrack shop and then hurriedly rush towards the bus stop to catch another bus which passes through their residential places.

In the case of monthly salaried employees, they usually go to their houses directly from their workplaces and visit the nearby arrack shops before they take their supper.

However, for the self-employed such as fruit and vegetable vendors, no such definite timings are reported as they have to continue their work till the traffic becomes thin or until their stock is over.

Drinking Practices and Reasons for Drinking

To elicit and describe the drinking practices the following indicators were considered: (i) frequency and period of drinking, (ii) quantum of drink per day, (iii) drinking alone or with company, (iv) dining together with his family regularly or not, (v) proportion of money they give at home out of their income, (vi) health and other problems due to arrack, and (vii) reasons for drinking.

Almost all the respondents are addicts to drink and have been drinking daily for the last one decade or so.

There are two types of sachets available in the market, viz., 45 ml. and 90 ml. No respondent is reported to be drinking less than 90 ml. quantity of arrack in a day. It is also observed at the shop that some of them purchase 2 packets or more containing 45 ml. each and consume one on the spot and the remaining at home. However, a minimum of 90 ml. is said to be a definite practice of drinking.

Drinking alone is a significant feature among the respondents. Almost all the participants expressed that question of drinking in company does not arise as they are already habituated to it. Further, the quantum of drink and the amount of money they spend depends upon their individual capacities. 'The more the earning the more will be the consumption' is the rule as revealed by them.

While the habit of dining together with their family members regularly is reported to be 100 per cent in the case of daily wage labourers, it is almost negligible among others since the nature of their work and timings of reaching home are different.

The proportion of income they give for household expenses is reported to be 50 per cent among the daily wage labourers and self-employed workers, while it is around 60 per cent in the case of monthly salaried employees.

The share of expenditure on drink and tobacco is reported to range between Rs. 10 and Rs. 20 for daily wage labourers and self-employed workers; while it is in between Rs. 500 and Rs. 800 per month for the Class-IV employees.

None of the respondents reported or seemed to be aware of any health disorder due to arrack consumption. However, other problems such as frequent quarrels with family members and neighbours, and meeting with minor or major accidents are reported in quite a large number. The above problems are observed to be higher among the monthly salaried Class IV employees as they frequently quarrel not only with their wives who insist on them to give up the habit of drinking but also with their colleagues at the work place in discussion on politics, movies etc. Further, among the other problems, taking petty loans for domestic purposes is found to be high in the categories of daily wage labourers and self-employed.

Most of the daily wage labourers report that they drink for relaxation. Their specific answers are: 'removes body pains,' 'gives sound sleep,' 'keeps fit for tomorrow's hard work,' 'feels active after having it,' etc. On the other hand, the reasons expressed by Class IV employees and self-employed drinkers are different. Their reasons are: 'family problems,' 'financial problems,' 'chronic health problems' and other 'mental worries.' However, a common reason expressed by almost all the respondents after some probing is addiction to arrack.

Attitudes Towards Prohibition

To know the attitudes of the respondents towards prohibition of arrack sales, the questions are: approval or disapproval of the respondents towards their own drinking habit and child drinking; their preference for regulation or total prohibition; awareness of and attitude towards women's movement; willingness to stop drinking if prohibition is imposed and reasons for unwillingness; alternatives in case of non-availability of arrack; and finally the nature of help required to give up their drinking habit.

Most of the respondents expressed disapproval of their own habit of drinking, very few justified their drinking. The reasons for disapproval are mainly: 'society dislikes drinkers,' 'wasteful expenditure,' 'leads to ill-health,' and 'frequent quarrels with family members.' The reasons for approval are: 'can't but,' 'working hard,' 'expenditure is less,' 'drinking less quantity,' etc.

Regarding their attitudes towards child drinking, all the respondents strongly disapproved of the habit of drinking among children. The reasons are: 'it spoils their future,' followed by 'bad habit' and 'society dislikes them.' However, some of the respondents continued to say that in the present days, children are also drinking and imitate their favourite cine actors.

A majority of the respondents are in favour of complete prohibition as they feel that as long as it is available in the market, they will go on purchasing it.

All the respondents are aware of the movement by women against arrack sales. Some of them also are aware that the selected shop was attacked twice before the survey by some agitating women of the nearby residential area. More than 50 per cent of the respondents were not sure of the sustainability and success of the movement.

When they were asked whether they could give up the habit of drinking, if prohibition is implemented, their responses were quite peculiar. Some of them reported that they might die if they stopped drinking abruptly. The other answers are: 'they can't consume food properly,' 'there may be sudden obsructions of nature calls; become unfit for working' and there may be other health problems. However, the common response observed is that they cannot give up drinking habit abruptly.

The respondents were also asked to suggest some alternative to drinking if prohibition is implemented. According to a large section of the respondents, arrack will definitely be available at some or other corner in the city even after prohibition though at higher prices. Some of the respondents said that they would go for cheap varities of I.M.F.L. such as brandy, whisky, etc., by sharing the expenditure between two or more like minded drinking partners. A small section of the respondents opted for toddy called as 'kallu.'

As regards the nature of help required, such as establishment of de-addiction centres, recreational centres and other measures that help to give up the drinking habit, all of them reported that they were not aware of such facilities so far.

Policy Suggestions on Prohibition of Arrack

The history of anit-liquor movement suggests that there is no particular or complete solution to this problem. A human system addicted for over a long period of time to a vice like this and with the associated psychological attitudes, needs strong exposures to educative and deaddicting programmes.

In the context of the strong possibility of illicit distillation and as spurious arrack is more injurious to health, part of the efforts voluntary organisations and women's movements should be directed towards prevention of illicit distillation.

If the Government decides against total prohibition, the following policy measures are immediately required.

(i) The Government should not issue fresh licences to arrack contractors.

(ii) The existing number of licenses must also be restricted to the lowest possible extent.

(iii) The number of arrack shops must be drastically decreased.

(iv) There should be restrictions on location of arrack shops near educational institutions, religious places, industrial areas, government offices, residential localities, national highways and other important places.

(v) Drinkers in a drunken state must not be allowed into workspots, transporting vehicles and other public places.

(vi) Arrack shops may be kept open within regulated hours only. The working days may also be minimised. Shops must be closed on pay days.

(vii) Drinking within the shop must be made compulsory.

(viii) There must be restriction on the quantum supplied to individual customers. Each drinker must be served a limited amount of arrack only.

(ix) The quantum to be sold by the shop-keepers in a day, must also be limited.

(x) Drink must be served to only those aged above 25.

(xi) The proportion of alcoholic contents per litre arrack may be reduced.

(xii) The Government may open recreation cells and the labourers may be supplied with cheap and nutritious food. However, care must be taken for proper utilisation of these centres by avoiding obscenities such as gambling, lottery, etc.

INDEX